2973 1027

3/04

☐ P9-BYM-318

How

WAL★MART

Is Destroying

America

(and the World)

WITHDRAWN

BEAVERTON CITY LIBRARY
Beaverton, OR 97005
Member of Washington County
COOPERATIVE LIBRARY SERVICES

How

WAL★MART

Is Destroying

America

(and the World)

And What You Can Do About It

Bill Quinn

TEN SPEED PRESS
Berkeley Toronto

Copyright © 2000 by Bill Quinn

All rights reserved. No part of this book may be reproduced in
any form, except brief excerpts for the purpose of review, without written permission of the publisher.

Ten Speed Press
Box 7123
Berkeley, California 94707
www.tenspeed.com

Distributed in Australia by Simon & Schuster Australia, in
Canada by Ten Speed Press Canada, in New Zealand by
Southern Publishers Group, in South Africa by Real Books,
and in the United Kingdom and Europe by Airlift Book
Company.

Writing assistance by Kristi Hein
Cover design by Lisa Patrizio
Illustrations by Ivar Diehl

Library of Congress Cataloging-in-Publication Data

Quinn, Bill, 1912 May 15-
    How Mal-Mart is destroying America (and the world) and
what you can do about it/Bill Quinn.—2nd ed.
        p. cm.
    ISBN 1-58008-231-9
    1. Wal-Mart (Firm) 2. Discount houses (Retail trade)—
United States. 3. Retail trade—United States—Personnel
Management. 4. Small business—United States. I. Title.

HF5429.2.Q56 2000
381'.149'0973—dc21   00-053518

Printed in the United States of America
First printing, 2000

6 7 8 9 10 — 07 06 05 04 03

To Lennie Quinn, my wife of fifty-four years, without whom I couldn't find my way to the bathroom.

To my son Rix, who took over the family publishing business twenty-two years ago and freed up the old man to write personal stuff, like this anti–Wal-Mart book.

To Phil Wood, president of Ten Speed Press, who shares my feelings on Walton Enterprises . . . and tells you why in his "Letter from the Publisher."

To Kristi Hein, San Francisco's most talented wordsmith, for polishing up this old man's prose for the one book on the market that's *over* 100% anti–Wal-Mart.

CONTENTS

In 1998 I proudly published the first edition of this book. At the time, I thought I was just doing my old friend, author Bill Quinn, a favor at the same time as I was getting back at a company that had caused us more than just a headache.

In 1995, Sam's Clubs, a division of the huge Wal-Mart Corporation, had bought almost 30,000 Ten Speed Press books, paying close to a quarter of a million dollars. Two months after we'd shipped them out, they sent back more than half of the order, requesting a refund for unsold merchandise. Worse yet, almost 70 percent of the returned books were so badly damaged, they couldn't be sold. Wal-Mart lacked a central warehouse so merchandise was sent back from individual stores, using whatever they had for packing material—in a couple of cases, that meant baling wire!

That first edition struck a chord in readers all across America, more so than we ever imagined or dreamed. It sold more than 20,000 copies. It also generated loads of calls and letters, helping Bill and his supporters establish and sustain a network of hundreds of people all over this country with a legitimate axe to grind against the Walton family empire.

Since that first edition, the picture hasn't gotten any prettier, at least as far as the business practices of the retail giant are concerned. As the title of this new edition indicates, Wal-Mart has spread its tentacles way beyond the borders of our beloved United States and is seriously threatening businesses and communities worldwide. In the meantime, back here at home, there are no fewer than a staggering 12,000 to 14,000 lawsuits currently pending against Wal-Mart.

We said it two years ago and we're saying it again: Read this book; marvel at Wal-Mart's audacity; then fight back. This book tells you how.

Every journalist—even the eighty-eight year-old who pens these lines—dreams of writing something that will make a difference in the fight against the evil dragons of the world.

One truly evil dragon is the giant discounter who has already crushed virtually all the mom-and-pop stores in America's small towns and has made huge dents in good-citizen stores like J.C. Penney and Sears in larger towns.

Maybe, just maybe, some readers of this new edition will step out of the shadows with a voice loud enough to curb the growth of the worst enemy American retailers and manufacturers of consumer products—and their consumers—have had in our country's history.

Yes, we know the odds are a million to one against us . . .

But what the hell. This is still America: the one place in the world where dreams can still come true.

Perhaps a little background on the author will put my anti–Wal-Mart crusade in perspective:

My dad was a small-town railroad agent who prided himself on knowing virtually everyone in the towns—three in Louisiana and four in Texas—where he worked. Pa Quinn finally settled in Grand Saline, down in beautiful East Texas, in 1920. (See map on page 15.)

He sank deep roots there, becoming a deacon in the Baptist church and an elected member of the school board. At the age of forty-six, he and my mother built their very first—and only—home.

The second of their two children, also known as me, inherited Pa's small-townitis and, at age fifteen, I announced to an unlistening world that I was going to grow up to be a newspaper editor. No one believed me, if for no other reason than that I had been the worst student in every grade to date.

Indeed, that ambition had almost faded by 1935, when, at the age of twenty-two, I was finally offered my first journalism job, as editor and publisher of the weekly Van (Texas) *Banner*. Salary: $60 a month. Van, by the way, had a population of about eight hundred.

By 1940, things were looking better. I became editor and publisher of my hometown paper, the *Grand Saline Sun*, serving a population of 1,799. Then I got a much better job, editing semi-weeklies in Mineola, a town of about four thousand.

In World War II, I served thirty-two months overseas. At first I was with the Third Infantry Division, then I moved to VI Corps Headquarters where I was named editor of a daily mobile newspaper started in Anzio, Italy—called, fittingly, the *Beachhead News*.

When I was discharged, I moved my old manual typewriter to Fort Worth and got into the trade journal publishing business. I continued to run our magazines in a highly personalized, country-newspaper style, making a better-than-average living until I finally retired—at age eighty-four.

But deep down inside, I never left "home"—Grand Saline, Texas. When someone asks me where I live, I still nod my head toward East Texas.

How's Grand Saline doing these days? There isn't a Wal-Mart there. Yet, only thirteen miles to the east in Mineola and thirteen miles to the south in Canton, Wal-Mart has superstores that have claimed well over half of Grand Saline's retail business.

Grand Saline once had three thriving independent dry goods stores. Now there's none.

The first casualty was a department store owned and operated by my wife's uncle for almost seventy years. The second was a department store that had to close its doors after being in business for over fifty years. The third locked its doors for good on New Year's Day, 1998. Other independent stores in the town have suffered proportionately.

It's been estimated that for each Wal-Mart store in existence, one hundred family-owned businesses have gone under. Which adds up to—what?—a quarter of a million mom-and-pop store owners tearfully telling their children that there will be no money if misfortune comes their way.

What really stirred me to first assemble stories for this book was a 1991 story in *Fortune* magazine. A *Fortune* reporter followed the late Sam Walton around for a week. His impression of the Arkansas genius:

> And finally, there is the ruthless, predatory Sam, who stalks competitors—in any *size, shape, or form* [emphasis added]—and finds sport in blasting them from the sky like so many quail.

Sam Walton's business principles laid the foundation for the ruthless corporation that has become the most feared retailer in American history:

✪ A company that got its start by building cheap, ugly, giant-size stores on the outskirts of small towns, and discounting prices so much that virtually every store in a once-proud downtown district had to close.

✪ A company that promised lots of new jobs to a small town—not bothering to tell the city fathers that most would pay near-poverty wages, and some 40 percent of the "associates" would work less than the customary forty hours.

✪ A company that, in the 1970s, promised that they would observe the century-old tradition of closing on Sundays . . . then, in the 1980s, hustled business during church hours . . . and later, stayed open 24 hours a day—forcing any remaining competitors to do the same.

✪ A company that promised that alcoholic beverages would never be added to their worries . . . and is now the largest retailer of "spirits" in the United States.

✪ A company that, to gain the support of small-town newspapers, started off as a good advertiser . . . then, once established, dropped virtually all newspaper advertising.

✪ A company that, to gain entrance to a new area, promised to become "part and parcel" of small-town America . . . and is now its worst citizen.

I'm not alone in my crusade, of course. anti–Wal-Mart campaigns have sprung up across the country. But fighting Wal-Mart is harder than David fighting Goliath. One way or the other, the Arkansas discounter squeezes its way in—often pressuring courts to decide in its favor.

After being successful in dominating small-town America, the bullies from Bentonville, Arkansas invaded small cities and bedroom municipalities surrounding metro cities with their Sam's Clubs and Supercenters.

The Wal-Mart juggernaut rolls on. If you've picked up a newspaper recently, you know that Wal-Mart now has a massive presence in Canada, Britain, Germany, and Mexico, and has made its first incursions into Argentina, Brazil, China, Korea, and Puerto Rico.

In the year 2000, the closely-knit Walton family owns a 38-percent interest in Wal-Mart that is worth almost $100 billion. But Walton Enterprises is showing no interest in slowing its greed. All we can do is hope that those with power, do something to get in its way.

Wal-Mart's strong anti-union stance became known in early Sam Walton days. Old Sam said he wouldn't be intimidated by unions, ever, under any circumstance. And today, with close to nine hundred thousand people working for Wal-Mart in America (and more than 200,000 work in other countries), not a single U.S. store is unionized. Chapter 3 does offer some recent heartening news of United Food and Commercial Workers [UFCW] victories in the fight to bring Wal-Mart meat packers union protection. It might be a small one, but it's a start.

Will this union—and others—mount a serious nation-wide campaign while there's still a chance?

City councils throughout the United States share a good deal of blame for the devastating effect Wal-Mart has had on almost every town and city it has invaded. The governing body of each municipality has a fair amount of power to slow or stop Wal-Mart.

They have plenty of weapons. Change zoning. Limit store size. Demand building architecture to fit the community. Require that all entrances be paved rather than hot-topped. Insist that Wal-Mart pay all expenses in building its own water and sewer lines and installing traffic lights. Levy a certain fee for excessive police calls from the store.

City councils everywhere should be on the alert . . . and line up the local legal talent to join the battle. City councils should certainly send members to surrounding towns that have Wal-Marts—or where Wal-Marts want to expand—to find out what Walton Enterprises is *really* "giving back" to the areas from which they are draining money. Will it take memberships in civic clubs and the chamber of commerce? Can

What Is Wal-Mart? ✓

It's the biggest retailer in the world. (It did *over $165 billion* in sales last year, worldwide. In our first edition, only two years ago, that figure was just $100 billion!)

It's the biggest private employer in the United States. As of May 5, 2000, 885,000 people work for Walton Enterprises in this country, more than 200,000 elsewhere, for a total of more than 1,000,000 employees worldwide.

With 3,020 outlets in the United States, it's a resident of virtually every town or city of any size. Another 1,019 outlets operate in Argentina, Brazil, Canada, China, Germany, Korea, Mexico, Puerto Rico, and the United Kingdom.

It's a predator. An article in *Forbes* magazine's 1991 "400 Richest" issue laid out the basic Wal-Mart concept as follows: "Discount stores in small towns and rural areas, each big enough to freeze out competition."

it be counted on to help finance the local hospital? Will it help underwrite school activities? *still low wages ok ?*

When will the state and federal governments take a look at one of the biggest cancers that has ever grown on American business?

Wal-Mart has already monopolized small-town America. Once a downtown crumbles, the state or federal government may be called in to pick up the pieces. Just one example: We understand that local school systems now obtain an average of only about 25 percent of necessary operating funds from their local tax base. The biggest culprits in dodging local taxes: Wal-Mart.

The Supercenter invasion is intended to make Wal-Mart the number-one grocer in the nation.

And that ain't all. Wal-Mart is now targeting small cities and metro areas in a big way. Sam's Clubs have been there for some time already. Now the bullies from Bentonville are test-marketing "Neighborhood Markets" of the fifty thousand square-foot variety they call "convenience stores"—complete with a pharmacy and fast-moving grocery items—in those last remaining non-Wal-Mart strongholds.

A government that saw Standard Oil and AT&T as monopolies ain't seen nothing yet.

Wal-Mart doesn't want just some of America's business . . .

THEY WANT IT ALL

If the Democrats and Republicans on Capitol Hill can ever stop sniping at each other, they might wake up to the serious threat posed by a company apparently without scruples; a company that's now not only the biggest retailer in the United States, but the biggest in the world; a company whose mushrooming size and power have permanently skewed not only the workings of America's "free market" system, but the global economy as well.

By the time Congress wakes up, the Wal-Mart colossus may just peer down at them . . . and laugh.

SEVEN BAD THINGS THAT HAPPEN WHEN WAL-MART COMES TO TOWN

Let's say it's your town. It's not big—maybe five thousand to thirty thousand folks live there, with all the businesses and services that would serve that many people. Probably, the town's not growing—and that worries some. Some think that a big retailer might help—something flashy to pull in people and money from a wider area.

So now, all of a sudden, there's a 155,000-square-foot "box" store out along the interstate, just barely inside the city limits—but definitely not "downtown." There's a sea of asphalt and a curtain of cyclone fencing where there used to be farmland or a trailer park or woods. Sam's in your town now, and he's ready to pull in the commerce from thirty-five miles around and more.

Here's what that will likely mean to you and your town.

BAD THING #1:
Store Owners Take the Biggest Hit

If you're a store owner, and your business is in direct competition with Wal-Mart (that is, you sell hardware, pharmaceu-

ticals, general merchandise, whatever), you already know you've got the fight of your life on your hands. Wal-Mart's sheer size gives it incredible advantages.

- ✪ Wal-Mart's arrival will probably be accompanied by a fair amount of excitement and anticipation. A lot of people in your town will want to have a Wal-Mart. They'll see all the advantages of having a big discounter around, probably without seeing the costs to the town and the life they have known.

- ✪ Because Wal-Mart is so darn big, it can cut almost any deal it wants with vendors and distributors (see chapter 3).

- ✪ Wal-Mart can lure your customers with claims of convenience and low prices (whether those claims are true is another matter—see chapter 4), offering an easy alternative to the downtown you and your fellow merchants have worked so hard to build.

- ✪ Wal-Mart can afford to spend quite a bit on advertising and promotion—and you can bet it will, at first. Read on to find out just how long that spending will last.

- ✪ Wal-Mart will engage in "predatory pricing" in an attempt to drive you out of business—fast!

A new Wal-Mart on the offensive against its local competition will be willing to take losses on merchandise that those competitors sell. It'll study what you sell, then offer it for less. Let's say you are Jim, and you own Jim's Hardware in your town. Local Wal-Mart managers will ascertain what you are selling and at what prices; then they will stock, advertise, and sell those items at prices near or below their cost. You can't possibly compete with this practice without losing

One State's Death Toll

★ A 1995 survey in Iowa showed what Wal-Mart had done to its state since arriving in 1983:

★ 50 percent of clothing stores had closed

★ 30 percent of hardware stores had closed

★ 25 percent of building materials stores had closed

★ 42 percent of variety stores had closed

★ 29 percent of shoe stores had closed

★ 17 percent of jewelry stores had closed

★ 26 percent of department stores had closed

Fast forward that 1995 survey to the year 2000, and we'd bet you can increase the above losses by at least 50 percent.

money, and chances are good that eventually you will be driven out. Wal-Mart will then be able to sell its hardware merchandise at whatever price it wishes, having eliminated the competition—you!

Wal-Mart takes its business overwhelmingly from existing businesses. Townspeople often hope that a big shiny Wal-Mart will pull in commerce from outside the town, thus bringing more money in. It will—but almost never enough to justify cannibalizing most of a small town's small businesses, which is what happens. On average, over one hundred stores eventually go out of business in the area surrounding a "Wal-ed" in town.

BAD THING #2: Jobs Are Lost

One of the biggest carrots Wal-Mart holds out to struggling small towns is the promise of more jobs. If a town is not

growing, this sounds really attractive: a great big new store is going to need people to work there, isn't it?

But, for every job created by a Wal-Mart, at least 1.5 jobs are lost, according to the Residents for Responsible Growth of Lake Placid, New York. Numerous other studies give similar figures. The biggest reason for this is that Wal-Mart is said to employ from sixty-five to seventy people for each $10 million in sales; other small businesses employ 106 people for each $10 million in sales. So Wal-Mart can do more business and pay less for employee salaries—and it will. This is one of the great cornerstones of Wal-Mart's success.

Also, a Wal-Mart or other big retailer coming to town is not really offering new jobs in the way a manufacturer would be. People sometimes lose sight of this. If a new factory opens in town, it is truly creating jobs that did not exist before; if a new store comes to town, and that store is selling merchandise that, for the most part, was already available in the town, it is just going to be rearranging the way money already gets spent in the town. What Wal-Mart offers is not *job creation*, but *job re-allocation* and, eventually, *job loss.*

It's also worth remembering that many of the jobs Wal-Mart offers are part-time and low-paying. Chances are that a vast majority of Wal-Mart's employees work fewer than the customary forty hours a week (the retailer defines a "full-time" worker as someone who puts in twenty-eight hours per week and above). And perhaps 60 to 70 percent of these workers (both full- and part-timers) have no health insurance. All are being paid a low retail wage, and all are subject to work shortage or layoff at the slightest downturn in store sales.

BAD THING #3: Other Businesses Suffer

Businesses that are not directly competitive with Wal-Mart (the ones that don't sell the same stuff) may have a kind of wary optimism about their big new commercial neighbor. Maybe, they think, Wal-Mart will share some of its wealth in town—sort of spread it around. Don't count on it.

NEWSPAPERS

When Wal-Mart first comes to a town, it may come to be known as a newspaper publisher's best friend. Full-page advertisements! Color inserts! The advertising money that Sam brings feels like a bonanza. But just you wait. As soon as the local drugstores and dry goods and hardware and appliance stores have closed, Wal-Mart may decide to withdraw almost its entire advertising expenditure from your pages. This pattern was first noted by *The Wall Street Journal* in a 1993 article.

A popular newsletter once cited two small newspaper publishers who had felt burned by Wal-Mart's abandonment:

❂ In one town in Arkansas, Wal-Mart promptly cut its local advertising down to the bone once it gained its desired market share. Wal-Mart then asked the local newspaper for publicity for its sponsorship of a local event. The publisher of the local paper, who had learned a bitter lesson from his former advertiser, told Wal-Mart to go to hell: "I don't give free publicity to companies that don't help pay the light bill around here."

❂ Another publisher—I believe it was in Snyder, Texas— was invited to come by and get a picture of founder Sam Walton when he came through the town. "Thanks, but no thanks," he told the Wal-Mart manager. "If we don't have a readership worth advertising to, why should you want us to run a photograph?"

Even in Sam Walton's own hometown of Bentonville, Arkansas, Wal-Mart rarely advertises in the local paper, according to a Wal-Mart director—and Sam's own son owns the paper!

Walter Buckel, publisher of the *Lamesa* (Texas) *Press-Reporter*, made weekly calls to the local Wal-Mart manager for many months, hoping for Wal-Mart advertising in his paper. This particular manager he spoke with seemed to take pleasure in brushing him off: "We're going with the mailers," he said.

Walter saw what was happening to his town and his long-established business friends . . . resulting in fewer and fewer ventures . . . and fired off a letter to the late Sam Walton. That letter has been passed around to fellow publishers who, like Walter, had the guts to fight back.

Walter's letter (too long to run in its entirety) truly touched on all the bases:

> In 21 years in business and a 47-year resident of Lamesa, I don't know of a single mailer company who

"We Don't Have to Explain Our Reasons"

According to the executive director of the Arkansas Press Association (APA), three members of the APA met with Paul Higham, Wal-Mart's vice president of marketing. Their mission: to persuade Wal-Mart to advertise in the daily and weekly newspapers they represent.

The APA members were big names in newspaper circles: Barry Newton, from the Oklahoma Newspaper Advertising Bureau; Julia Jackson, from a group of newspapers in the southeastern United States; and Dennis Schick, APA executive director. As Shick tells it, they arrived expecting a private meeting with Mr. Higham. Instead, they were met by four media buyers—all relatively young, and two of them brand new at Wal-Mart.

After several minutes, Mr. Higham appeared, asking why the three of them were there. It soon became apparent he was not overly glad to see them. For the next two hours, Higham delivered a "canned and rehearsed" spiel, including these pronouncements:

★ Newspaper (advertising) costs too much to buy.

★ Newspapers have poor and decreasing quality news–editorial content.

★ Newspaper profits are too high.

The APA group asked: "Why does Wal-Mart on occasion advertise in one newspaper—and not in another very similar newspaper?"

Higham's response: "We don't have to explain our reasons for doing what we do."

What, then, can a newspaper to do to earn Wal-Mart's business?

"We don't need you or anyone else to speak for us. We'll do it ourselves."

One of the APA trio walked out of the meeting muttering, "He's the most arrogant and rude person I've ever dealt with."

has ever contributed a penny or even given a thought to Lamesa. They bleed us—and give nothing back.

I regret Wal-Mart supports only this kind of (advertising) operation.

We like to think we are community builders and give back a generous amount of what we take out.

We have a paid circulation of 4698 that covers our trade territory with over 80 percent penetration.

(Compare the 80-percent coverage with the Wal-Mart mailer that comes with other junk mail!)

I don't ever recall a mailer hurrying out to a Wal-Mart store with a camera to give your local store a front-page news story.

We've always been there when you needed us.

Wal-Mart needs to support REAL AMERICA— and it starts with hometowns like Lamesa, Texas.

To destroy us with absolute support for mailers is to destroy the very thing that we were led to believe Sam Walton believed in.

BANKS

We've been told that it's part of Wal-Mart's overall business strategy to instantly transfer its daily earnings from its stores directly to corporate headquarters in Bentonville, Arkansas. So, while the local bank may have accounts with Wal-Mart, the retailer is just using the bank to drain cash from the town: pour the dollars in, then pipe them out of town the next day. The bank never gets to use the capital this cash might represent, and, what's worse, the town doesn't get any benefit from it either.

One rule of thumb states that every dollar spent in a small business will get spent again one or more times before it leaves the area (more if there are not a lot of tourists and other outsiders coming into and out of the area). This means that when a dollar is spent at Wal-Mart instead of at the local hardware store, not only does the hardware store lose that dollar in revenue. Also losing might be the local hauling company that delivers to the store or the cafe where the store manager has dinner. Instead, that dollar goes directly to the Walton family's private Fort Knox in Bentonville, where it rafts up against billions of other bucks from around the world.

Seen from a larger perspective, Wal-Mart's nonrelationship with local banks can stunt a town's overall growth. Small towns often rely upon their banks as engines of growth: this is where capital meets investors and new businesses are formed. But if capital is hopping on the morning flight to Arkansas every day, entrepreneurs (that is, potential employers) are left empty-handed, and they'll have to just go away or give up.

TOURISM

Is your town a charmer, like historic Sturbridge, Massachusetts, or Gig Harbor, Washington? Do people come from outside the area to revel in your town's ambience? You may really want to think two or three times about whether Wal-Mart's big old prefab one-look-fits-all box store is going to be what those free-spending tourists want to see.

In Lake Placid, New York, local citizens did a survey to see what tourists and visitors thought about the proposed Wal-Mart in town. The results:

✪ 94 percent of respondents said they would be disappointed to see a Wal-Mart in Lake Placid (3 percent would be pleased; 3 percent had no opinion).

✪ 95 percent said a Wal-Mart would detract from the appeal of Lake Placid (2 percent said it would add to the appeal; 3 percent said it would not affect the appeal).

✪ 72 percent said a Wal-Mart would make them less likely to visit Lake Placid again (2 percent said it would make them more likely to visit; 26 percent said they had no opinion).

"Stomp the Comp"

Ever since the first years of the Wal-Mart chain, we've been hearing that its "associates" (i.e. workers) are pep-talked into believing that to keep their jobs, they must fight all those independent businesses in town—who are out to destroy Wal-Mart(!).

"Dominate! Dominate!" the folks at Wal-Mart headquarters have preached to their managers and department heads from day one.

Certainly in the early days, there was a Wal-Mart "us against them" attitude, even though Wal-Mart's competition was then, for the most part, small-town mom-and-pop stores. Nowadays, though, Wal-Mart would rather present a kinder, gentler image. You know: "We love our communities. We're good neighbors. There's plenty of room for other retailers here."

But a phrase coined way back when—"Stomp the Comp!" (the competition, that is) has persisted, even into the end of the 1990s. In Ticonderoga, New York, a Wal-Mart employee allegedly secretly snapped a picture of a "Stomp the Comp" poster in the employees' lounge and gave it to the manager of a Great American store—one of the five retailers targeted by Wal-Mart's price-cutting arrows.

What happened to Great American?

Sadly, Wal-Mart's "Stomp the Comp" campaign worked.

Clear enough?

(By the way, all three of these towns—Sturbridge, Massachusetts; Gig Harbor, Washington; and Lake Placid, New York—have successfully fought off Wal-Mart's approach to their towns—mostly through the organized work of outspoken and tenacious citizens, and sometimes after very hard battles indeed. Your town can do it too: see chapter 7.)

BAD THING #4: Downtown Dies

This is the all-too-frequent result of Wal-Mart's infiltration of a town—and it's part of the plan. Wal-Mart's formula is to provide a neatly packaged and heavily promoted alternative to downtown.

It is an essential part of Wal-Mart's expansion plan to choose a site that is not within the downtown area: Wal-Mart builds on undeveloped land away from both a town's established center and/or business district. Moreover, Wal-Mart's developer normally buys the land at the cheapest possible price, and the land is graded and hard-topped expressly to accommodate itself—not to fit in with a town's larger development plan or work in partnership with other businesses in town. Wal-Mart knows where it wants to be and how it wants to operate—not in proximity to other businesses, and not in partnership with other merchants. Wal-Mart is there to destroy the competition and make a buck, not to build community or add to the one that exists.

Wary local activist groups have done studies on what would happen to their local economies if a Wal-Mart came in, and the results are chilling (though not surprising). The Save Historic East Aurora (New York) Association projected that a new Wal-Mart in their town would "strip our retailers, and especially our Main Street business district, of 68 percent of their existing sales" . . . Scary!

BAD THING #5:
Taxpayers Pay for the Disaster

These big retail boxes take up a lot of a city's resources—
streets, water, sewer lines, power tie-ins—and a lot of these
services would have to be newly provided because Wal-Mart
is, in its ideal plan, building on undeveloped property. You can
bet, with Sam's eye on the bottom line, that he is not going to
quietly pay for what he uses if he can stick it to somebody else.

Indeed, the *Portland Oregonian* reported that when Wal-
Mart opened its store in Lebanon, Oregon, "Things heated
up at the city council when Wal-Mart 'suggested' the city
make some improvements to its streets, water and sewer tie-
ins, and add some traffic lights—a package that was estimated to cost a half-million dollars." This suggestion, remember, was from a discounter who was going to ship the
dollars made in Lebanon right out of town the morning after,
rarely pausing to invest anything in the town that recently
rolled out such a plush red carpet for it.

The Planning Board of New Paltz, New York crunched
some numbers on what would happen in their city (fiscally
speaking) if they let Wal-Mart build a Supercenter in their
town. Here are their enlightening findings:

Wal-Mart property tax	+$100,000
Cost of municipal services	-$29,000
Cost of additional services	-$5,000
Tax losses at three other malls	-$29,000
50 percent property tax abatement	-$50,000
Total town tax deficit	<$13,000>

So, at this conservative estimate, the town would actually
come out losing $13,000 a year. This does not even begin to

account for other losses brought about by stores closing, people losing their jobs, and the flight of local cash right back to Bentonville. You may not be surprised to learn that New Paltz decided not to allow the proposed Wal-Mart in their town.

In addition, there are probably any number of other, hidden costs attached to Wal-Mart's coming to town, and some of them may be difficult to predict or notice before it's too late. For instance, the town of North Elba, New York, according to the Residents for Responsible Growth in nearby Lake Placid, is allocated a certain amount of hydropower at a fairly inexpensive rate. With the coming of a Wal-Mart into their municipality though, the demand for electric power would probably rise significantly—and so would the price. With one new corporate citizen (that is, Wal-Mart), North Elba would be using far more than its allocated power, and everyone's rates would go up significantly.

Do you think this cost was accounted for anywhere in Wal-Mart's proposal to come to North Elba? I doubt it.

Local Law Enforcement Feels the Strain

One other cost the town will have to contend with when Wal-Mart opens is that of the increased need for law enforcement. A number of small-town police departments have been speaking out about the unforeseen increase in their workload. Wal-Marts are almost always on the outskirts of their municipalities. And while the stores draw customers from a wider radius, the town's cops and courts are the ones who have to deal with the increased number of disturbances a big discount outlet attracts. "We've had more than our share of problems down there," says William Enright, chair selectman of Avon, Massachusetts. "It costs the town a lot of money in court time."

BAD THING #6: Other Towns Suffer

It's not just towns that actually have a Wal-Mart within their city limits that feel the negative effects on their commerce and quality of life. But then again, that's all part of the plan. The sales area of a Wal-Mart is about seventy miles in diameter, and one of Wal-Mart's corporate strategies is to "carpet" the land. This means that essentially the entire country falls within the sales area of at least one Wal-Mart. So it stands to reason that a number of towns will lose commerce to a nearby Wal-Mart without getting much of anything in return. Take my hometown of Grand Saline, Texas (population 3,000).

I grew up there. In the '20s and '30s (and '40s and '50s and so on), a person had to actually look for a parking space downtown. Now it's almost empty—and it's even worse on Saturday, which used to be the busiest shopping day of the week. The city sales tax revenue took a 54 percent drop over a twelve-month period. The First National Bank went out of business. Once there were three drug stores, three thriving dry goods stores, three stores selling appliances. Now: one, none, and none, respectively.

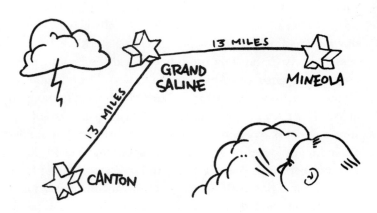

Grand Saline doesn't have a Wal-Mart, but Mineola and Canton—both only thirteen miles away—do. Grand Saline's own businesses have sickened and died and its downtown has shriveled. Grand Saline is becoming a commercial suburb of the Wals in Mineola and Canton. It's hard to watch this happening to the town I love!

BAD THING #7: Wal-Mart Moves On

Even scarier are the tales of woe from the towns that actually were strip-mined by Wal-Mart. A small town's lifeblood isn't always enough to feed the world's largest discounter—not any more. Consider the story of Nowata, Oklahoma— brought down not once but twice by Wal-Mart's policies of expansion and consolidation.

Nowata is an oil town of about four thousand souls in north central Oklahoma. In 1982, Wal-Mart came to town and quickly became the "new downtown." According to an article in the *New York Times*, a collapse in world oil prices and the typically splashy opening of the superstore combined to drive roughly half of the local shops out of business. For over ten years, Wal-Mart was the city's biggest business and, with seventy employees, its second biggest employer.

Then, in 1994, Wal-Mart left, and the city of Nowata was shattered again. This was a town that had sacrificed its business diversity to the "box," and had quickly come to depend on the presence of Wal-Mart in town. The citizens of Nowata, disproportionately poor and elderly, loyally shopped at Wal-Mart, keeping its revenues healthy: An analysis of the store's sales tax payments in the early '90s shows that, on average, the residents of Nowata were spending over $1,200 a year per person at Wal-Mart. Bryan L. Lee, president of the First National Bank of Nowata, where Wal-Mart made night deposits, has said that daily receipts for the store were as

"They are just trying to kill everybody else."

The Fort Worth *Star-Telegram* ran a story in early January 2000 that just had to disturb every business person in the Dallas/Fort Worth metro area—one already oversaturated with discount stores.

The Bentonville blankety-blanks, who already have about forty stores in this area, announced plans for fifty new stores over the next few years. This adds up, according to the Telegram, to over *five million square feet of additional selling space*.

Meaning, of course, the "death" of a thousand or more small independent businesses in this part of Texas.

Jim Whitten, a retail broker for CB Richard Ellis, has this observation:

"They are in a big-time growth mode. THEY ARE JUST TRYING TO KILL EVERYBODY ELSE [emphasis added]."

So . . . we just have to ask this question . . . again:

How big is too big?

strong and steady right before the store closed as they had ever been in the store's history.

So what happened? It seems the good citizens of Nowata—like those in a growing number of Wal-Mart towns across the country—got caught in the next phase of Wal-Mart's growth strategy: "consolidation." In short, the construction of a new Wal-Mart Supercenter in Bartlesville, thirty miles from Nowata, meant that two older and smaller Wal-Marts—the ones in Nowata and Pawhuska, to the south and east—had to go. And the folks who used to shop at those two smaller stores now had to travel to Bartlesville to get their tennis shoes and plastic tackleboxes. (For more about Wal-Mart's Supercenter "consolidation" strategy, see chapter 6.)

For Nowata, Wal-Mart's pullout felt like disaster all over again. A lot of people were thrown out of work. Many folks who didn't have cars lost the only place where they could do some of their necessary shopping. And, due to lost sales tax, city officials were left scrambling to bridge an $80,000 deficit in the city's 1995 municipal budget of $1.2 million. To cope, city manager Nancy Shipley was forced to lay off city workers, cancel projects, and raise taxes: Water and sewer taxes climbed 32 percent.

More than anything, the town felt betrayed: Wal-Mart had come in, made itself necessary, then left without notice. Indeed, right before the store closed, Wal-Mart in Nowata posted signs outside: "The rumors are false: Wal-Mart will be here always." (When asked about these signs, Don E. Shinkle, Wal-Mart's vice president for corporate affairs, said that they were put up "based on market research at the time, and the later decision [to abandon the stores] was based on market research later." How's that for firm, reliable corporate policy?)

In some sense, you could say that this is the way things are: Businesses sometimes leave and deliver a crippling blow to the communities they abandon. This is part of the cost of doing business. But in a town like Nowata, cruelly cut down twice by the same massive retailer, that cost is too high, especially when it seems to be paid by the folks with the most to lose.

For the story of Hearne, Texas—another Nowata—see page 125.

WE GET LETTERS . . .

A SLICE OF LIFE LOST

There will be no more make-your-mouth-water-just-by-looking-in-the-display-case apple pies at Brandon's Hillcrest

Make Us an Offer!

We're flat-out *stunned* to find this wide-open window on yet another branch of the Bentonvillains' global takeover scheme. Here's what you'll read when you go to: www.wal-martrealty.com:

> You know us as a retailer.
>
> We are also a Real Estate Company.
>
> We sometimes outgrow the buildings that house our retail stores and, when we do, we look for ways to utilize our real estate to benefit other end users, Wal-Mart, and the surrounding community.
>
> Wal-Mart Realty Company is uniquely qualified to provide a complete real estate service to your company. We have existing buildings located throughout the United States. Furthermore, we have the capability of providing demographic information on our locations and can close your deal in a timely manner. Not only can we offer you guidance in the selection and acquisition of your site, we also have architects, engineers, and tenant construction managers who are capable of moving a project from the ground breaking to grand opening. You will find that our buildings are extremely versatile and can be converted to fulfill almost any business need. In addition, these locations offer plenty of parking in a prime location.
>
> Outparcels and sometimes large tracts of land are available near our Supercenters, Sam's Clubs, and Wal-Mart stores across the U.S.A.

When we visited the "Buildings" page, we were charmed by the before-and-after shots of a once-abandoned Sam's Club, now reborn as . . . a Mercedes-Benz dealership! Isn't that just what's been missing from your hometown?

Market in Alliance, Ohio. No more homemade apple, cherry, pecan, pumpkin, rhubarb, blueberry, lemon meringue, coconut cream, chocolate, or banana pies to tempt the taste buds. No more Hillcrest cookies or specialty cakes for birthdays and other happy occasions—all made from the very finest ingredients.

In his letter to us, store owner David Brandon points his finger at the Wal-Mart's cut-rate pastry department as the villain in the closing of his store's "best bakery in this town of 25,000 people."

Oh, sure, people were still coming to the Hillcrest bakery for those special desserts families want on Christmas and Thanksgiving and birthdays—but special-day purchases alone weren't enough to attract folks away from Wal-Mart's flashy "Always Low Price" sign.

It's equally disturbing that Barb Moser, the much-beloved head baker at Hillcrest for the past thirty-three years, will no longer be there. After a farewell that left the store managers and Barb in tears, she has been forced to go searching for another job.

David Brandon enclosed a front-page newspaper story of Barb leaving the best job she ever had, with this headline:

A Slice of Life Lost

He adds:

> The blanketing you refer to in your books is happening . . . a giant Wal-Mart here . . . another 25 miles west in Canton, Ohio . . . another one is being forced onto the city of Salem, located 25 miles to the east.
>
> I only wish I could have read your books sooner.

DOWN AND DIRTY

Wal-Mart's recent suit against Amazon.com—charging that the bookseller lured Wal-Martians away from Arkansas for much better jobs with Amazon in beautiful Washington state (see page 47)—amuses my friend Rollie Helmling. Rollie, who owns and operates three state-of-the-art supermarkets in and around Vincennes, Indiana, writes:

> We are still open and still making a profit, but in the last three years since they opened a Supercenter and have tried to drive us out of business, I have aged ten years.
>
> Until you have experienced competing with them, you don't have any idea how vicious this animal is.
>
> You are right on target: Wal-Mart is destroying lives, livelihoods, neighborhoods and entire communities.

During a telephone conversation, Rollie talked about how dirty Wal-Mart can get in doing what they said Amazon had done to them.

Rollie has lost employees in the most underhanded way: Wal-Mart departmental managers have come to his store at off times, like late on Sundays, when fewer of his own managers are on duty. His employees tell him that they offer his staffers a dollar more per hour and promises galore to come over and be "associates" at Wal-Mart.

Rollie has gone a step further in battling the blankety-blanks from Bentonville: He's ordered boxes of this book and is giving copies to members of the Vincennes City Council, influential friends, and of course, his own key people.

You may want to contact Rollie to see how his battle against the dirty discounter is progressing:

Rollie Helmling, Harold's SUPER markets,
1400 Washington Ave., Vincennes, Indiana 47591
Tel. 812-882-0191

. . . AND WE GET CALLS

AN UGLY TORNADO

Bryan Wickert of Viroqua, Wisconsin dialed up on July 27, 1999. It seems that Wal-Mart is trying to build one of its Supercenters in this town of about four thousand—a move that could completely destroy the few mom-and-pop stores that have survived a smaller Wal-Mart outlet.

The Supercenter's big grocery department, plus a bigger stock of everything, would make it by far the largest store in the area—which would, in turn, wipe out scores of other independents within a twenty- to thirty-mile radius of Viroqua.

Bryan added a little more to his picture:

> Every time I pass by our local Wal-Mart—or a Wal-Mart store in any other town—I visualize an ugly tornado dipping down and wiping out every town and every dollar in the area . . . dollars blowing straight into Bentonville . . . never to return. Ever.

EAST SIDE, WEST SIDE, ALL AROUND THE TOWN

It's almost unbelievable the extent to which Wal-Mart will go to dominate the retail scene in whatever town or city they target.

Shortly after the first edition of this book came out in 1998, I had a call from Norman, Oklahoma—a small city of about sixty thousand within sight of Oklahoma City—telling me that Wal-Mart, which already enjoys a good business there, wanted to expand.

"In what way?" I asked.

"Well, now, they want to add two superstores of about 200,000 square feet—each. One on the west side of town, the other on the east side."

My caller explained that the business people in Norman had protested and, as I understand it, the city put up some roadblocks—but Wal-Mart met the challenge. It paid for a street to be built to the back of its proposed store on the west side, and said it would also put up its own stoplights.

The city council must have folded, for in writing this bad news, I understand Wal-Mart opened a 225,000-square-foot Supercenter on the east side in May 1999, and that the west-side Supercenter opened for business that December. So, poor Norman now has about 400,000 square feet of new Wal-Marts.

Wal-Mart estimates its per-square-foot sales at $385, which adds up to about $150 million lost business for other Norman stores—and, conservatively, a loss of over one hundred tax-paying Norman independent businesses.

The old, smaller Wal-Mart store that's been in Norman all along? It's closed, of course. We note, too, that Wal-Mart's online realty, www.wal-martrealty.com, shows five plots for sale in Norman—each about an acre, and four at the same street address. Could just be a coincidence.

2

ONE SURE-FIRE WAY WAL-MART BARGES INTO TOWN

(AND THREE WAYS IT SNEAKS IN)

Sam Walton claimed that one of his bedrock business principles was never to build in a town where Wal-Mart was not wanted. This was probably an easier thing to do way back in the day when Sam and Company were just beginning their pattern of world domination. Back then, towns didn't know what they were inviting in, and what Wal-Mart was selling sounded pretty good.

By the 1990s, things had definitely changed; dozens of private anti–Wal-Mart groups had sprung up throughout America. The majority of these are citizen activist groups in specific small towns where Wal-Mart has planned a store. Some of these groups have taken their messages on the Internet (see chapter 7, "Fight 'em in Cyberspace"), and many of them have received a fair amount of visibility in the national press. The word is finally getting out about Wal-Mart's effect on a community, and the retailer is finding more and more towns that say, "We don't want you, Wal-Mart!"

But, in the words of New York developer John Nigro, who has worked to bring Wal-Mart into some of its targeted towns, "[the big retailers] know what they want." If Wal-Mart wants to come into your town, and it knows just where it wants a store to sit, Wal-Mart will come to town even when faced with a helluva fight—even when faced with towns that do not want Wal-Mart and say so.

BARGING IN WAY #1:
Location, Location, Location

To paraphrase the old real-estate saw about what makes a property desirable, there are really only three things Wal-Mart needs to move into a town:

(1) Zoning,

(2) Zoning, and

(3) Zoning

Strike Three

I'm delighted to see a *Bloomberg News* report that the Vermont Supreme Court turned down Wal-Mart's third attempt to put in a store in St. Albans, Vermont. The court says it "was proper for the state to consider the store's likely harm to competitors."

The court went a step beyond the above statement, ruling "that state law allowed the board to consider competition (like Wal-Mart's) as part of a project's impact on health, safety, and welfare. The closing of rival retailers would hurt local government's ability to raise taxes to provide services."

The dry (very dry) laugh I get from all this is in harking back to Wal-Mart founder Sam Walton's pledge that he would never put a store into a town where it was not wanted. Just think: Wal-Mart, after three rejections, was still trying to bully its way into St. Albans!

The master plan for Wal-Mart, wherever it goes, involves the "box": the classic Wal-Mart square, prefab, ugly monstrosity of a building surrounded by asphalt parking lots as far as the eye can see. Uniform architecture and site-planning is one of the keys to the retailer's scary success. No surprises; every place is the same. It's like mass production.

When Wal-Mart wants to come into a town, it fixes its eye on a certain parcel or parcels of land that will fit the bill: undeveloped and outside the downtown or other business district, with plenty of room for parking and easy access by the highway or other major roads.

Often, Wal-Mart will find its dream parcel, but it's not always zoned for the kind of heavy-duty retail use Wal-Mart wants it for. So Wal-Mart has to get the zoning changed before or at the same time that it applies for a business permit. Often this is not such a big task. Wal-Mart and its developers are pros at this, and have prepared documents that show the city council and the planning commission that Wal-Mart will be the best new citizen of the town imaginable, and that this parcel of land was made to be Wal-Mart's new home. (These proposals tend to be studded with what one Wal-Mart critic has dubbed "Wal-Math"; that is, "they only know how to add": more jobs, more community involvement, local buying, positive response to local needs—the whole phoney-baloney ball of wax.)

Understandably enough, for people who don't want a Wal-Mart in their town, this is the best stage to stop it. The Lancaster County (Pennsylvania) Planning Commission put together a succinct summary of the steps small towns should take in "Wal-Mart-proofing" themselves. (Thanks, folks. This is dry stuff, but useful as hell.)

✪ Adopt urban growth boundaries; in other words, limit the area in which urban-level development can happen within the town, and make those boundaries clear.

✪ Review local comprehensive plans; a town's comprehensive plan is a document that sets out the goals and policies for a town's desired growth pattern. This is a town's statement of what it is and what it wants to become, and it can be a powerful document in fighting outside developers who have their own ideas about what should become of the town.

✪ Review zoning ordinances; a town's zoning ordinance should be consistent with the town's comprehensive plan.

✪ Review subdivision and land development regulations. These regulations specify what a developer must demonstrate about the nature and impact of its proposed development. Make sure the regulations are strong and detailed enough to give your town a clear picture of any proposed development—from the developer itself.

It's not so easy anymore for Wal-Mart to just waltz into a town with its usual bag of tricks. The words "Wal-Mart is coming" are like a red flag for lots of citizens who have seen what havoc the monster retailer has wreaked in other towns—and who don't want any such thing happening to their town.

Wal-Mart has had to evolve some ways to get around this new defensiveness. God forbid it should just say, "Oh, okay, small town, you don't want us, so we'll go elsewhere." I've pinpointed three of Wal-Mart's sleazy ways to weasel its way into your town—all sneaky as can be.

SNEAKY WAY #1:
Manipulate Existing Zoning

In Virginia, Wal-Mart was able to come up with an absolutely ingenious way to get around not one, but two sets of municipal codes at once. Here's what happened. In the town of Warrenton, the city code said that any retail outlet over fifty thousand square feet had to have special permission to be built. When the Wal came to Warrenton, it naturally had to ask for such permission to put in its proposed monster: a 120,000-square-foot box. Properly alarmed at the thought, the city said no, that's just too big for us. On the face of it, Wal-Mart was beat: they asked and got turned down.

Now, Fauquier County, which surrounds the town of Warrenton, has a similar code on its books, stating that retail outlets exceeding seventy-five thousand square feet have to be approved.

But voila! Wal-Mart found an appropriately zoned parcel that straddled the line between Warrenton and unincorporated Fauquier County, and the discounter was able to get around both sets of restrictions by putting less than fifty thousand square feet of its box inside Warrenton land, and less

Here's Your Hat—What's Your Hurry?

In one county, the discounter wanted to take over a mobile home park occupied by 170 residents so it could build a 136,000-square-foot supercenter. The company's original offer to the residents if they'd relocate? Two hundred big old American dollars. "This isn't fair," said one resident who had lived on the site for four and a half years. No, my friend, it's not.

Dateline North Carolina

T. R. Taylor and his wife wanted a house away from downtown that they could settle in for life. They found the perfect spot back in 1940—a one-and-a-half-acre wooded plot. They built their house and cleared some trees to make a garden. Decades went by before their dreams were shattered. The Taylors now have a Wal-Mart built around them, ruining the property they have been on for sixty years. Wal-Mart bought the land next to theirs and bulldozed around their house, leaving them twenty feet up a bank, with a ditch thirty feet across and three hundred feet long separating their property from the superstore. An insulting offer was made for the Taylors' property—an offer that they turned down. Even the line of trees that was supposed to buffer the house from the development never materialized. The Taylors' son sums it up thusly: "Human beings do not do this to other human beings."

Does Wal-Mart Hold Nothing Sacred?

A friend in Hawaii faxed us a front-page story in the *Honolulu Advertiser* several years ago about Wal-Mart trying to build "on land that should have gone to long-suffering Hawaiians who have been on the waiting list for homestead lands for decades." You can bet that Wal-Mart will get out its slime buckets and throw every possible drop at anyone and everyone who crosses it in building one of its box stores on land that rightfully belongs to Hawaiian natives.

than seventy-five thousand square feet on Fauquier County land, for a grand total—still—of over 120,000 feet! Local courts found that the use was permitted—or at least was not excluded—by the available laws.

Thirteen neighbors of the proposed Wal-Mart development appealed the ruling that said this arrangement was legal. One of them, Deborah Gortenhuis, said in an interview with the *Washington Post*, "I think it's sort of sneaky that they want to do this thing. Wal-Mart tries to depict itself as this very honest, family-oriented, small-town kind of store. But with all this sneaking around, you wonder about that. It seems ruthless."

SNEAKY WAY #2: Use a Front Man

This is a damned effective technique. From what I can see, it's one of Wal-Mart's favorites. Check it out.

Some aware citizens in Evergreen, Colorado, suspected that Wal-Mart was scoping out their town for a possible location. They called Wal-Mart headquarters several times and asked them what its development plans were for Evergreen. Each time the reply was the same: "We are not looking at real estate in Evergreen."

Wal-Mart Is No Longer Welcome, Says North Fort Worth Neighborhood

The real estate developer's sign reads "Ninety-eight acres for sale."

Ninety-eight acres of hell, if Wal-Mart has its way of disrupting yet another happy community.

"Once Wal-Mart was welcome, but not any more." So say many, many, many Fort Worth North Side folks—plus at least six neighborhood associations—to the threat of Wal-Mart building one of its monster Supercenters smack dab in the middle of single-family homes . . . across the street from a high school . . . near five other schools . . . and at the intersection of two, two-lane streets.

When the local TV news talked to neighbors in March 2000, their comments ranged from surprise to anger:

"We never dreamed this would happen when we built our home here," said a newly-married lady. A mother worried: "This additional traffic will make our neighborhood a hundred times more dangerous."

"Our quality of life will certainly be changed for the worse," said another mother.

A well-known businessman found the Wal-Mart supermarket proposed for the site "totally out of scale."

Meanwhile, a real estate development company from Denver appeared before the county zoning board, asking for rezoning on a couple of parcels. They don't own the parcels, but are interested in getting them rezoned, then acquiring them for later sale or lease to Wal-Mart. In this way, the path will be paved for Wal-Mart to come in, and local citizens who would wish to keep it out have lost one of their most powerful weapons in the fight: strict zoning restrictions.

Institutional Racism?

A fellow Wal-Mart hater brought up store placement a year or so ago, pointing out that he had never run across a Wal-Mart store in a predominantly minority area. Now comes vindication of his observation, a story with a St. Louis dateline: "A black businessman and a minority-rights group said . . . they have sued Wal-Mart stores in federal courts, charging the nation's No. 1 retailer with discrimination in store placement. They accuse Wal-Mart of retail redlining, which involves closing stores or not opening new stores in predominantly black neighborhoods."

Check out the racial breakdown in the area of the Wal-Mart nearest you. It might surprise you.

A similar sort of thing recently happened in Arroyo Grande, California, where Wal-Mart, when asked, repeatedly said it had no plans to come. At the same time, a developer was pushing through the necessary zoning changes for an unnamed store, denying to town officials all along that their client was Wal-Mart. The developers were busted when a citizen came forward with a copy of a sell/lease agreement signed months before by Wal-Mart and the developer.

Yet again, I hear that the city council of Ithaca, New York unanimously voted to spend $3,600 in outside lawyer fees to keep Wal-Mart from building a store just inside the city limits. Seems a development company from South Carolina, working on Wal-Mart's behalf, had secured a conditional zoning variance from the city to build "an unidentified store." When the city found out the store was to be a Wal-Mart, they said no. Now they are fighting to keep the Wal out of their town.

Let this be a warning to would-be Wal-Mart busters: keep an eye on rezoning requests that would make a parcel Wal-Mart-ready, *no matter who has submitted the request.* You don't know who's really behind it.

SNEAKY WAY #3: Hell, Use a Straw Man

This is the only time I've heard of Wal-Mart using this particular tactic, and I can see why. It sure is not the kind of situation a big old strong international conglomerate retailer wants to find itself in more than once—embarrassing!

In Greenfield, Massachusetts, Wal-Mart was facing quite a battle from a grassroots citizens' group that wanted no part of the retailer in their town. In what can only have been a state of desperation, the retailer set up a phony citizens' group called "The Citizens for Economic Growth," which started

Papa Sam's "Creation" Disrespects the Father of Our Country

Does Wal-Mart respect any rule of decency? When it announced its plan to build a supercenter on George Washington's old Ferry Farm where, 'tis said, he chopped down that cherry tree, a residents' group begged the retail giant to build elsewhere and, instead, donate the site for historic preservation. "This is very naive," said Jay Allen, Wal-Mart's vice president for corporate affairs. "We're going ahead."

running pro-Wal-Mart ads in the newspaper. When the anti–Wal-Marters called to find out who was on this new citizens' committee, they got no reply. A little further sleuthing revealed that "The Citizens" were (1) Wal-Mart's lawyer, (2) her secretary, and (3) her secretary's boyfriend.

Well, maybe Wal-Mart only abandoned this type of ploy because it got caught at it so darned easy. Pathetic!

3

TWO WAYS WAL-MART IS OH SO GREEDY

I'd like to start this chapter out with parts of an interview I conducted with a former Wal-Mart manager; a man who had been on the inside of the beast for over fifteen years. A lot of what Joe [not his real name] has to say speaks to the top Two Ways Wal-Mart Is Oh So Greedy.

BQ: Joe, your wife tells me your hours as a manager were so long you barely knew your children?

Joe: Long hours were demanded—rarely less than seventy a week, most weeks eighty or more. Days off were rare. And I have gone as long as three years without a vacation. My wife literally raised our children by herself.

BQ: Hourly workers, I've been told, are held to a minimum?

Joe: You won't believe how they are treated. Managers try to keep employees' hours under twenty-eight a week so they won't be eligible for benefits.

If business slows on any day, managers are instructed to send workers home any time after they have four hours on the clock. Even department heads who are supposed to be regulars can be sent home, ofttimes working less than the eight hours they are entitled to.

BQ: Is it better now than it was?

Joe: No, worse, I've been told. When a regular employee quits now, managers are instructed to hire two part-time people to take his or her place.

BQ: This is a personal question, and you may not want to answer it. But how much did you make as a store manager?

Joe: You'll laugh at this. But before I quit in the 1980s, I made $15,000 a year, but I could draw up to $15,000 against my annual bonus, which I normally had to do. Most I ever made was $35,000. And I was considered one of their better managers, constantly on the upgrade, getting better stores.

BQ: When you moved, did Wal-Mart pay your expenses?

Joe: No. Actually, the "system" was to ask store personnel to do you a favor by working off the clock to come out to your place and help you pack. You were moved to your next assignment, always, in a Wal-Mart truck. And at your new sta-

tion you asked for volunteers to come out and help you unpack. Never on company time. Always off the clock.

BQ: What about real estate you might leave behind?

Joe: Wal-Mart headquarters always bluntly told you they were not in the real-estate business. Had never been. Would never be. And, on our next-to-last move, we took a helluva loss on our home.

BQ: Suppose you told your regional manager you were happy where you were and didn't want to move?

Joe: That wouldn't work either. It was always a larger store, paying a little more. But in spite of that, I told my boss one time I wanted to stay where I was. Then I got a call from the vice president of stores from my area to suggest, in the strongest terms, that I start packing. It was as simple as that. If I refused, I was out the door, fired, through with my future at Wal-Mart.

Why didn't I quit? I've asked myself that a thousand times. But one gets to doing something, knows he's good at it, and feels, ultimately, that things will get a lot better. I don't know why I didn't get the hell out sooner, but when you've got a family and lots of years invested, you just stay with the company.

BQ: In traveling from place to place, the company paid car expenses, didn't they?

Joe: That's another area where Wal-Mart is chintzy. Chintzy beyond belief. My mileage refund on one of the years I remember was 11¢ [a mile]. My wife was working at the time, and her company car allowance was 22¢ a mile. Double my allowance!

BQ: I've heard that when you had annual meetings to which your wife was invited, they wouldn't allow you to use your own car?

Joe: That's another not-so-funny joke. I remember a couple of those widely-touted "family" affairs the company called "Wal-Mart Ballyhoos." Always by bus.

Four or five managers would drive their own cars to a central Wal-Mart store, load up, travel on to the next central pick-up point, pick up another group, and so on until the bus was loaded to the gills. We went up to one meeting in Missouri that was a fourteen-hour bus drive. Got up at 5:00 A.M. to catch the bus. No stop for lunch. And, everyone was required to bring their own sack snacks. Once there . . . tired, tired, tired . . . no refreshment bar.

Then two days of intense meetings, 7:00 A.M. until almost midnight. Then, on the fourth day, back on that damn bus for home. And on that fifth day, you had better be back to work—on time.

On another of these trips they said it would be at the rather nice Hot Springs Majestic Hotel. Not for us. It was something like a Day's Inn, and a long, long walk to the Majestic, where our meetings were held.

BQ: When you opened a new store, what happened?

Joe: We were instructed to go into a town to dominate! Dominate! Dominate! First job was to shop the competition. I had a full-time person to do my "dirty" work for me. I particularly remember [town name deleted].

My lady shopper would come back with their prices, dictated into a hidden microphone. We'd cut their prices a penny or two. If we got into real warfare with a Kmart or Target, we'd send our people over to their stores to buy as many of their sales items as we could . . . and brought them back and sold that product for a little less. We even shopped the mom-and-pop hardware and drug stores. Our job was to destroy the competition, large and small, in every way we could. If a mom-and-pop store couldn't stay in business—their problem. Never, never was there a more ruthless bunch of blankety-blanks than Wal-Mart.

BQ: Were you encouraged to belong to local civic organizations?

Joe: Yes. We were encouraged to join and be as much a part of that organization as possible, but always at our own expense. I was never reimbursed for any of the money I spent that way. But, for sure, Wal-Mart emphasized that their key personnel were a part and parcel of their respective communities.

BQ: What about charitable contributions in the towns you were in?

Joe: Wal-Mart had a simple strategy for that. When someone came in for a contribution, you welcomed them with open arms and told them store policy was simple: Just write a letter on their organization's letterhead, and you'd be glad to send it to company headquarters that very day. A week or two would go by, and, if asked, you'd tell the solicitor that, "Well, you know how long it takes a request to go through the channels in a company as big as Wal-Mart." Then, a couple of months later, all would be forgotten. The job of the manager was to be nice, nice, nice to those people who come in for a contribution to their cause.

BQ: I've heard awful stories about how mean Wal-Mart can be to its vendors.

Joe: That's one of the reasons I had to quit them. I had one lady whose main job was to make claims of product damage, or claim that the full order was not received, pallet damage, whatever. The company's policy was to make a vendor prove the full order was sent. On damage, they had to believe our claim—or lose Wal-Mart as a customer. You can't believe the number of claims an average Wal-Mart store makes in a single year. Not one store. All stores.

BQ: What about local vendors?

Joe: When we bought from a local vendor, except for utilities, of course, we were instructed to deduct 10 percent. Don't ask me for what. If we had to call in someone to service something, same thing. Quite often the invoice would be held if there was the slightest question. Normally, the local vendor would allow us to take the 10 percent. I was against all this—to the fullest. But those were our instructions.

Let me add here that all of those petty claims against virtually all vendors were not written instructions, always verbal. So far as I recall, I've never seen anything written on Wal-Mart stationery on which they might face suit.

BQ: What part of your job was most unpleasant?

Joe: Being responsible for hiring personnel. And working them just as cheap as you can get by on. My guess is that the Wal-Mart employee of today is even worse off than he was some thirty years ago, when I went to work for them.

I'd say that eighty percent of their workforce is in the minimum wage area. I think you'd be surprised how many of them are on food stamps or some other assistance.

BQ: Newspaper friends have told me that when a new store goes in, they're good advertisers, but once the store is in, advertising levels off.

Joe: I know that for a fact. They go all-out to beat down the competition, demand certain positions in the local paper, use fractional pages with no other advertising on the page. They know every trick of the trade. Demanding, demanding of everybody.

But once they dominate the competition, it's usually a once-a-month circular or insert. NO NEWSPAPER COULD EXIST IF ALL THE STORES IN TOWN WERE LIKE WAL-MART [emphasis added].

BQ: What was your worst experience at Wal-Mart?

Joe: Being sent into a town with instructions to fire the key people—often for petty infractions of company policies. Things like that tug at your heart.

BQ: When you finally quit Wal-Mart, were you fully vested?

Joe: I thought so. I calculated I had $30,000 coming. But you can't believe the deductions they added to my final check. Administrative expenses, deductions I never dreamed of. The final amount was only $5,000. I should have sued, but that would have entailed legal expense, and like all claims against Wal-Mart, it would have been in the courts forever.

BQ: What was your actual reason for quitting?

Joe: My conscience was eating me up. My normal weight is around two hundred pounds, and I was down to about 145. My deepest concern was that I was selling every moral I ever believed in.

BQ: Would you say Wal-Mart is dishonest?

Joe: I don't know how to answer that. I do know they take advantage of virtually everybody who has ever worked for them. I do know that they take every advantage of their vendors. I do know that they take advantage of every customer who walks into their store.

My greatest regret in life is that I ever tied up with Wal-Mart in the first place. And I know in my heart that if you interviewed every former manager of Wal-Mart, the vast ma-

---

Clean-Up the Parking Lot: Will the Nearest Shopper Please Assist?

This from a September 1997 feature story in *The Wall Street Journal*: "Wal-Mart in Irving, Texas has posted signs on its doors asking customers to bring in a shopping cart from the parking lot. For their troubles, shoppers can enter a weekly drawing for a $10 gift certificate." Note it's a weekly drawing, not a daily one. One $10 prize! Wow! How can a family worth almost $100 billion afford to share their riches so generously?

jority of them would tell you an almost identical story [to this one] I'm telling you today.

So, without further ado, here are the two biggest ways I've found that Wal-Mart Is Oh So Greedy:

GREEDY WAY #1:
Employees Are Wrung Dry

You've heard the war stories of one former Wal-Mart manager, Joe, who gave so many years of his life to a company he now regrets ever hearing of. Sadly, Joe's story is not unique: Many Wal-Mart employees ("associates," as they are called) are honorable, capable, hard-working folks. It's too bad their big boss pretty much sees them as bumps on his bottom line.

It is widely acknowledged that one of the great keys to Wal-Mart's formidable success is its lower-than-low cost of doing business. Wages in particular are as low as can be. Every gear in the whole vast machine is straining to keep costs down, profits up, and growth exploding. Of the hundreds of places Wal-Mart can (and does!) save money, its workers' hides are the favorite.

Minimum wages and minimum benefits: that's the way Wal-Mart stays ultra-competitive. Here are a few more "features" of working for the world's largest retailer:

LOW PAY, SCANTY HOURS

Retail jobs pay the least of all categories of employment tracked by the U.S. Census Bureau: lower than service, lower than mining, certainly lower than manufacturing. These wages are approximately 39 percent lower than the average wage, and a full-time retail wage normally puts the earner well below the federal poverty line. So the people who work at Wal-Mart are not looking at the rosiest picture to start with.

Caught in the Act!

Wal-Mart can be so nasty to its employees that you just have to scratch your head and wonder how some Wal-Mart executives can sleep at night, knowing how some of its so-called "associates" are treated. This actually happened at the Wal-Mart store in Monticello, Kentucky:

The January 1, 1999 *Wall Street Journal* tells the tale of four female employees—all approaching their seven-year anniversaries with the company—who were "caught in the act" by the store's video camera. All four were promptly fired. Their crime? Munching nuts and mints from damaged vendor packages while working on the floor.

The women took their case to court. There, "The tapes showed the four did eat a small amount of nuts and mints. The employees, however, maintained they were following an unwritten policy in which such food was left in lounges for employees and managers to consume."

The jury deliberated for less than ninety minutes before awarding them $5 million apiece—a total of $20 million .Wal-Mart was "considering an appeal."

It gets worse. According to the United Commercial Food Workers union, Wal-Mart workers make an average of $3 per hour less than unionized supermarket workers, $2 per hour less than other supermarket workers, and $1 per hour less than the average retail wage earner.

Then, remember that many Wal-Marters work part-time (the company doesn't release employment data, so we don't know how many). Now realize that Wal-Mart defines "full-time" as twenty-eight hours per week or more, and you'll see a workforce where the actual majority does not work a regular, forty-hour work week at all. Many—too many—Wal-

Leaving So Soon? I Wouldn't Hear of It!

Seems as though if you're a Wal-Mart employee, either you don't get to work enough hours, or you have to work too many—there's just no happy medium. As a result, many quit—creating a tremendous turnover rate even when compared to the retail industry as a whole. According to a clipping sent by one reader (unnamed, but it sure looks like *The Wall Street Journal*):

> That's the upshot of cases involving employees of . . . Wal-Mart stores forced to stay at their job sites without pay during lunch breaks.

> Wal-Mart . . . agreed to pay 933 Connecticut workers $325,192 in back wages, settling a state enforcement action seeking pay for night restockers who aren't allowed to leave stores during meal breaks.

Mart employees must be on food stamps or other government assistance.

This reality can be a bitter pill for folks in some towns who welcomed Wal-Mart and its promise of additional jobs. Wal-Mart will hire you, all right, but you may not be able to afford to shop in the store very often.

THE DISPOSABLE WORKER (I)

Even "full-time" Wal-Mart workers have no job security: none, zippo, zero. As reported in an article in *Inc.* magazine's July 1994 issue, regular employees are subject to having their hours cut any time, any hour of the day, whenever business slows down. Managers are under pressure to keep staff

Wal-Mart Ordered to Pay Ex-Worker $50 Million in Sexual Harassment Case

So hollered a headline from my local paper that deserves to be passed on. It happened in Warsaw, Missouri. Pamela Kimsey and two other women who still work at the store testified that their supervisor and other male employees pinched and kicked them. Wal-Mart will appeal, of course, and the abused ladies will be lucky to get more than "time off" money in the final settlement.

levels in line with the flow of business, and often this is done on the fly, midshift. Makes it a little hard to plan the old household budget, doesn't it?

And if business overall slows down? Well, in the words of one of its suppliers' reps, Wal-Mart operates on the basis of sink or swim; and it doesn't care if you sink. Just keep hoping that Bentonville HQ doesn't shut down your whole store.

THE DISPOSABLE WORKER (II)

In Plattsburgh, New York, Wal-Mart opened a brand-new store around the Christmas holidays in 1993. By the end of January 1994, the company had laid off thirty of its new employees—a mere month after the opening. These people had not known that they were just being offered seasonal jobs. Happy Holidays from Wal-Mart!

ROTTEN BENEFITS

When Wal-Mart personnel managers recruit eager new employees, they make much of the company's benefits.

How good are they? Not very, according to our calculations.

Let's take retirement—the 401-(k) plan. According to *The Wall Street Journal*, a survey found that "Wal-Mart stores reallocate forfeitures to remaining plan participants." This means that some contributions originally destined to aid young, lower-paid employees end up benefiting longer-service, higher-paid employees.

At Wal-Mart, for example, it takes *seven* years for an employee to become fully vested (that is, entitled to the employer's contributions). That's the maximum period allowed by law for a graded vesting schedule. (By way of comparison, at our old company, Quinn Publications, employees were vested after one year.)

"In 1997, for example, 70,268 of the 464,725 participants in the plan left the discount retailer before hitting the seven-year mark," according to *The Wall Street Journal*. That's one in seven leaving money in the pot!

When a *Wall Street Journal* reporter asked Wal-Mart to comment on the larger-than-average mass exodus, the Bentonville spokesman declined to talk about those less-than-desirable numbers.

What about medical benefits? The United Food and Commercial Workers Union's Web site, www.walmartwatch.com, shows just how bad Wal-Mart rates in the matter of health-care coverage for its employees: it's the lowest of the low.

The company's euphemistically named "Personal Choice" health plan charges such huge premiums and high deductibles that barely 38 percent of employees can afford coverage. The retailer also requires that, to be eligible for coverage, an employee must work at least twenty-eight hours per week (remember, twenty-eight hours per week is Wal-Mart's definition of "full time") and have been employed at Wal-Mart for at least two years. So that means the 30 percent or more of Wal-Mart employees who are part-timers aren't eligible at all.

Then, on average, Wal-Mart employees pay close to *half* the cost of their health plan—much, much more than the national average, which is 28 percent, according to the UFCW.

It's no wonder, then, that so many Wal-Mart employees must look elsewhere for their health-care insurance. A Wal-Mart spokesperson has admitted that "[Wal-Mart employees] who choose not to participate in [Wal-Mart's health plan]

Amazon.com, Inc. Is One Company that Ain't Taking No Crap from Wal-Mart . . .

It all started in 1998 when Wal-Mart sued Amazon, accusing it of "improperly recruiting Wal-Mart employees and misappropriating their proprietary knowledge." Amazon's chief information officer, Richard Dalzell, one of fifteen former Wal-Mart employees now working for Seattle-based Amazon.com or Drugstore.com, was quick to fight back:

"Wal-Mart has suffered employee morale and labor problems for the last few years, and there are several web sites dedicated to the problem."

So Amazon.com filed a counter suit accusing Wal-Mart, among other things "of filing the original suit in an attempt to prevent other Wal-Mart employees from leaving and to buy more time to develop Wal-Mart's own faltering online offering."

Amazon's counter suit also states that it had made job offers to only about 10 percent of the Wal-Mart employees who approached the Seattle company, suggesting that 150 Wal-Martians offered their services to Amazon. A Wal-Mart spokesman didn't dispute that figure.

Promises, Promises

They're made to break. At least the U.S. Equal Employment Opportunity Commission is likely to believe that about Wal-Mart.

The EEOC long ago ruled that it was illegal to screen out disabled job applicants through a questionnaire. Did Wal-Mart think that it could get around that with this slick approach: asking whether new applicants "might need any accommodations to perform required duties."

The EEOC's Sacramento, California office quickly responded by filing a suit against Wal-Mart for trying to avoid hiring workers who might have some sort of a disability. EEOC attorney David Kelley says Wal-Mart immediately assured the commission they were no longer using the form.

Kelly followed through to see if Wal-Mart was living up to its promise. The answer: Nope!

"We learned through our investigation that they continued to use it in various facilities in California, Texas, Arizona—and elsewhere."

usually get their health-care benefits from a spouse or the state or federal government."

Think about it. By handing off the expense of providing health insurance to over 500,000 of its employees—to responsible employers and taxpayers—Wal-Mart benefits to the tune of $1 billion annually, according to the UFCW.

Speaking of the UFCW, they've provided some of the few good-news items on the Wal-Mart front since our first edition. Many of the folks who work at the big grocery chains are card-carrying UFCW members. So Wal-Mart's Supercenter invasion—with its direct threat to the grocers, and all those underpaid "associates" toiling without union protection—has been like a red flag waved in front of the union's nose. Read on for the good news. . . .

WAL-MART WORKER VICTORIES

JACKSONVILLE—THE TURNING POINT? What one person can do!

Maurice Miller, a forty-five year-old barrel-chested meat cutter at the Wal-Mart store in Jacksonville, Texas (population: 12,765), was making only about $11 an hour at this grueling job after years of experience in his craft . . . and he wanted a raise.

Maurice knew for sure that he was being vastly underpaid. Union meat-cutters at Kroger stores in the area were making $14.66 an hour, $13.29 for apprentices. Plus they were getting paid health insurance (Wal-Mart employees pay for about *half* of theirs; see page 47), dental insurance, and vision care.

So, knowing that he was making much less than comparable meat cutters, he continued to request a $2-an-hour raise. His supervisor finally agreed. But when the day arrived for the raise to start, the supervisor turned him down flat.

Maurice got mad. Real, real mad. He turned to the United Food and Commercial Workers Union in Grapevine, Texas for help.

Shawn Barkley, regional director of the UFCW, sent down one of his best men, Brad Edwards, to see what he could do. What a challenge!

Unionize a Wal-Mart? Are you crazy? A company that is anti-union to the core, that had defeated the union at every turn? Not a single Wal-Mart in the U.S. was unionized. And East Texas? In the labor movement, a unionized Wal-Mart store there was about as likely as a man flying to the moon—on his own wings.

But Maurice and Brad didn't give a damn about what the naysayers were predicting. Together, they accomplished something that may go down in the history of the labor movement.

Brad set up headquarters in Jacksonville in September, 1999. He had his boss' permission to take it slow and easy. One small step at a time.

Maurice and Brad agreed that for a first vote they would target the only true college-degreeless craftsmen in the store—the meat cutters. Pharmacists, who must have at least five years of college, could come later.

Fast-forward to February 2000. A vote was finally called. Only ten were declared eligible, as full-time meat market workers.

The vote?

For a union: 7

Against a union: 3

A gigantic 70 percent victory! A clear win for the unions.

Wal-Mart, true to its anti-union past, is appealing. Once the union is in, though, you can imagine how the other Wal-Mart employees in Jacksonville will feel every time they pass the meat department and know that the folks behind the counter there are making $4–$5 per hour more than they are. This could be the start of something big. . . .

Back to Brad's organizing. As you can imagine, it was a helluva fight from start to finish. Early on, Wal-Mart, predictably, tried to move company zealots into the meat market. The union protested to the National Labor Relations Board. It won.

There was speculation that Wal-Mart threatened to have pre-cut and wrapped meat from a central market brought in.

Reportedly, it threatened to withdraw an annual store bonus of a few hundred dollars (usually $400–$500), and also to cancel the pension program for the meat department.

But, wisely, the meat cutters ignored that and other threats.

Now he's getting calls from Wal-Mart people everywhere, wanting to know how to organize.

There's also hope for another segmented group of Wal-Mart employees—perhaps the most abused Walton workers of all: the pharmacists (see the following section, "Victory for Wal-Mart Pharmacists").

Bottom line to these first small victories:

"Any time you get a toehold or a foothold, it is significant," says professor David A. Larson, 45, an expert of labor law and dispute resolution at Hamline University School of Law in St. Paul, Minn. "It's sort of like scaffolding or cracking the citadel. People will hear about this and get empowered. And if it happens in a place like Texas—a right-to-work state not historically sympathetic to labor—they will think they'd have a respectable chance anywhere."

VICTORY FOR WAL-MART PHARMACISTS

Abuse of pharmacists—who practice one of the most respected professions in the world—should be a penitentiary offense. Unfortunately, it's not. And, unfortunately, the courts didn't catch Wal-Mart until a Denver judge ruled in August 1999 that Wal-Mart had long violated labor laws by not paying overtime and must pay back wages.

Consider what we know as standard for the industry: Our favorite pharmacy, owned by a Fort Worth-Dallas family-owned firm, pays pharmacists strictly by the hour—and time-and-a-half for overtime. And the half-dozen or more pharmacists we've known the past couple of decades, all employed by reputable organizations, have had comparable relations with their employers.

Wal-Mart, so far as we know, is the only major discounter that takes exception to the pay-by-the-hour rule. The Arkansas discounter argues that its pharmacists are salaried employees, not hourly workers, and should not get overtime pay or compensation for working over forty hours.

The Denver judge thought otherwise, saying in its summary judgment that Wal-Mart treated its pharmacists as hourly workers by telling them to go home when business was slow, and docking their pay accordingly. The pharmacists also argued that they worked many hours off-the-clock doing paperwork and filing insurance claims for customers . . . often working sixty hours a week instead of their scheduled forty hours.

Some seven hundred pharmacists were involved in the lawsuit, and another four hundred current and former Wal-Mart pharmacists who missed the deadline for joining the class are covered in another class action suit, says the attorney for the group.

Each pharmacist is owed $50,000 to $75,000, according to Gerald Bader, a lawyer with a second law firm representing the pharmacists.

Now, here's the fun part: Attorneys say that Wal-Mart would have to pay $100 million in back pay, including interest. That figure doesn't include other damages, and a court decision could order Wal-Mart to pay missed wages for an additional year if it rules that the discounter intentionally shortchanged its employees.

One final thought: If Wal-Mart doesn't respect its pharmacists—a profession in which errors can be a matter of life and death—how little, how very little respect it must have for the rest of its "associates" (not to mention its customers!).

Viva Las Vegas!

When Wal-Mart announced it would be bringing its Supercenters into Las Vegas, in Nevada's Clark County, in the fall of 1999, the county commissioners were listening.

Knowing that a Wal-Mart Supercenter includes a full-size grocery department, Clark County—whose jurisdiction is the law in about half of the Las Vegas metro area—has adopted a land-use law that limits the amount of space that discounters who "sell everything under one roof" can devote to groceries: this can be no more than 7.5 percent.

The ordinance does not mention Wal-Mart by name, and it could apply to other "big box" discounters such as Target, Kmart, and Costco. But its prime target was unmistakably Wal-Mart.

The city of Las Vegas (the other half of Clark County) is expected to follow suit and vote in a comparable edict.

Labor unions gave birth to Las Vegas and have kept their clout down through the years. The casinos are nearly 100 percent union. All or nearly all the big grocery chains like Krogers and Albertsons are unionized. All are paying good wages—with a lot of company-paid benefits.

If one of the worst enemies of labor in the history of U.S. retailing tries to bring its cut-throat tactics to Vegas, we wager it's in for the nastiest fight in its history. The Walton family—long known for its lowdown, dirty fights with its competition—is likely to learn a long-deserved lesson.

When you kick labor unions, they kick back. Harder. A helluva lot harder.

WE GET LETTERS . . .

WAL-MART? TRUSTWORTHY? THE HELL THEY ARE!

A Wal-Mart computer specialist—who quit to avoid having a nervous breakdown—was so teed off that he wrote us a five-page, single-spaced letter. Some of his charges are "old hat" to those of you who might have talked to someone who has worked for the Walton Enterprises' headquarters in Bentonville, but if you want to sharpen your anti–Wal-Mart ax, read what our ex-Wal-Martian says he went through:

Like all former employees, he prefers that we don't mention his name, for "I am truly fearful of them and don't want them to destroy my life by harassing me." In essence, here's why he quit his job, paraphrased from his letter:

✪ The Wal-Mart people who hired me promised me a career and a review every six months, so I took a cut in salary from my old job. They did not honor this promise.

✪ I was told I would be working on certain types of computer technologies. They did not honor this promise.

✪ Once a month, on the first Wednesday, they require you go to a divisional meeting where you must do Wal-Mart cheers. How silly to watch forty and fifty year olds doing this.

✪ All "associates" are required to wear ID badges which they say they want you to wear at all times to get fellow Wal-Mart employees to "know you better." What they don't tell you is there are badge watchers all over the place. They even know how long you were in the bathroom . . . and which bathroom it was.

✪ There are cameras all over the place: those black half-bubbles that protrude from the ceilings and are around every corner—believe me, even your small cubes are within view of the cameras. They also have security people watching you all the time.

✪ You must report to work by 7:30 (no exceptions) and cannot leave before 5:30—but you can work beyond 5:30 . . . but many, many times our supervisors gave us impossible deadlines, requiring you to stay as late as 10:30.

✪ About those six-month reviews. I never got mine.

✪ Christmas bonus? Heavens no. Instead, a cheap Christmas season lunch. And I do mean cheap.

✪ Employee are prohibited from using all electric items like fans in the summer (often needed) and heaters in the winter (very, very often needed). They call them fire hazards. Who are they trying to fool? They simply save the Waltons thousands of dollars on electricity.

✪ What they don't tell you is that, during the Christmas holidays, you are required to work at least 8–10 hours a day in a Wal-Mart store . . . often as much as 100 miles away.

✪ When I quit, I had to have an "exit" interview. And before I could leave, I had to empty my pockets and show them the contents of my briefcase.

ANOTHER FRONT-LINE REPORT

Carolyn Gravely of Berkeley, California, writes movingly of her experiences as a Wal-Mart employee, including her fearful moments of working the "graveyard" shift (midnight to eight A.M.). According to her letter, the manager ordered her group to park on the outskirts of the parking lot to save space for customers. Then they heard that, to save electricity, Wal-Mart would turn off the lights that illuminated those areas "after normal evening shopping hours."

But what she said happened to other employees was even worse:

> If employees were caught stealing, they were paraded through the store for everyone to see.
>
> I saw two young stock boys fired on the spot for eating a piece of candy out of a bag which a customer had already opened.
>
> I worked across the aisle from a truly model employee who fell while stocking a very tall shelf, hurting herself, and then [was] told she couldn't sue because she wasn't authorized to be up there.

And to think the late Sam Walton demanded that employees be referred to by the much warmer word—"associates."

GREEDY WAY #2: Suppliers Are Squeezed

Wal-Mart has a lot of clout: a nice fat order from this mega-retailer would seem to be the dream of many manufacturing concerns. Wrong, wrong, wrong!

Because Wal-Mart is so big, it can (and does!) demand just about anything it wants from its vendors, anything from deeper-than-usual discounts to downright disadvantageous shipping policies to enforced returns on slow-moving merchandise. Some manufacturers are getting to the point where they just say "no" to doing business with Wal-Mart: the huge sale is not worth the even huger headache.

I can well remember how shabbily Walton Enterprises treated manufacturers' reps in the early days. And it looks even worse when you consider that those same reps played a big part in Wal-Mart's expansion from a small regional chain to the nation's No. 1 retailer.

Back in the '60s when we were publishing national trade journals for the outdoor power equipment and bike industries, reps often took long drives from their homes in Kansas City, Dallas, Memphis, and other far-flung cities to get relatively small orders from Wal-Mart headquarters in Bentonville (*always* for immediate shipment). Orders so small that, in some instances, the commission didn't cover the rep's trip expenses.

The Bentonville buyers often demanded special favors—like merchandise donations for store openings—or financial contributions when Wal-Mart agreed to feature that rep's product in a special sale. The reps we met at trade shows were constantly confronted by other discounters, demanding the same special treatment that Wal-Mart was getting.

Those reps had the feeling that they'd better be at new store openings when Sam Walton himself cut the ribbon. Be there—or else! The reps had to pay those trip expenses themselves. And more often than not, those openings were held on the weekend—forcing them to be away on days that rightfully belonged to their families.

Then, boom! In the 1980s, Wal-Mart announced that it would no longer deal with reps. Instead, it would place orders only with a vendor executive. This came at a time when reps were just beginning to see a profit from the one "down-home" company they had truly felt would be with them always.

With friends like Wal-Mart, who needs enemies?

Here are some of the other things Wal-Mart does to its vendors—so often that these practices begin to feel like unwritten policies.

CLAIM SHIPMENT DAMAGE WHENEVER YOU CAN

Remember my interview with Joe, the former Wal-Mart manager who finally quit after over fifteen years? He told me how he had one "complaint" employee whose main job it was to claim product damage, or to tell vendors that the product was not received or that the pallets it came on were damaged.

Dog in a Manger

This is a story about a small business in Texas that thought it could coexist with Sam. It was wrong.

Hot Diggity Dog, a hot dog vendor owned by a woman named Scarlett Rabelais, was doing all right. Between 1987 and 1991, Scarlett had contracted with Sam's Wholesale Clubs to sell hot dogs outside eleven Sam's stores in Texas. Scarlett gave Sam's 10 percent of the gross sales for the privilege of setting up outside its doors, and she bought the food for Hot Diggity Dog from Sam's Club.

According to radio commentator Alex Burton, the problem came when Hot Diggity Dog started making some money. Sam noticed and said he'd like to buy out the company. Scarlett said no, and Wal-Mart ordered the vendor off its land.

Here's the kicker. Scarlett's ninety-two employees were all elderly or handicapped people who would probably be on welfare if not for their Hot Diggity jobs. That Sam Walton would be willing to throw these people out of business because he couldn't get all the profit from their work shows just where his idea of community and social responsibility is: not one step over his own bottom line.

What was that you were saying about the cost of welfare being too high, Mr. Walton? Would you care to do anything real about it? Didn't think so.

In fact, this policy—forcing vendors to prove they sent their full order of merchandise—was the one that may have finally made him feel he had to leave Wal-Mart. And when Wal-Mart claimed damage (which was often), vendors had to take Wal-Mart's word on it—or lose a huge customer.

Quite by accident, I once overheard a conversation that

seemed to imply that there may be something a bit fishy about Wal-Mart's damage policies. Two food brokers from different companies had sold to the mega-retailer; and both were evaluating whether they were actually losing money by doing so. The reason? Wal-Mart's tendency to deduct alleged damage on shipments. They are "worse than all the others put together," said one of the brokers.

U.S. WORKERS SOLD DOWN THE RIVER

How much does Wal-Mart care about buying American? These two paragraphs from Al Norman's *Sprawl-Busters Alert,* July 1997, answer that pretty well:

In Newburgh, New York, the Wal-Mart store was picketed by members of the Professional Workers Association after 290 workers were laid off by the Hudson Valley Tree Company. It seems Wal-Mart canceled its contract with the American manufacturer of artificial Christmas trees. Hudson Valley Trees says that it lost its contract because Wal-Mart, which boasts of its 'Buy American' program, opted instead to purchase artificial trees from China.

According to the AFL-CIO, late last year a Native American (Indian) company went out of business on the St. Regis Reservation in northern New York after Wal-Mart decided not to carry its fishing lures. Officials at the Mohawk-owned Kanenkeha Lure Company urged a boycott of Wal-Mart. Kanenkeha employed eighty people at its peak.

PENALIZE VENDORS WHEN MERCHANDISE DOESN'T SELL

The National Apparel Bureau has gotten wind from its members that Wal-Mart has been forcing an extra discount from

> ### Some of Wal-Mart's Tricks for Wringing Out a Few More Bucks (according to Business Week)
>
> ❂ Calling a supplier collect
> ❂ Asking for huge numbers of free samples
> ❂ Asking for discounts for new store openings
> ❂ Commissioning cheap knock-offs of successful brand products
>
> . . . and so much more!

them on merchandise that doesn't sell. The Bureau's president says he has received "numerous complaints from vendors [saying] that the discount retailer was demanding a 'markdown allowance' of between 4 and 10 percent [for merchandise] Wal-Mart purchased from them but couldn't move . . . and [using] the threat of reprisals, including ending their business relationship, if vendors didn't comply."

You may want to circle the above paragraph and send it to folks in your industry who are selling to Wal-Mart or Sam's Club. If they haven't gotten caught in this slimy practice yet, they're probably just lucky.

CANCEL ORDERS IMMEDIATELY WHEN BUSINESS SLOWS

Vendors tell me that when sales reports tell the headquarters in Bentonville that sales are weak, Wal-Mart is notorious for canceling orders or refusing shipment on orders right away. This disregard for manufacturers is the sort of thing that can send smaller or less-prepared suppliers into serious trouble— even bankruptcy—on Wal-Mart's whim.

From the Pulpit

Sam Walton and Wal-Mart, ever my nominees for the scum of mass-merchandisers, are getting criticized even in the pulpit down in my part of the country.

A preacher here in Fort Worth, Dr. Barry Bailey, senior minister of the ten thousand member First Methodist Church for some sixteen years, had a several-minute segment on the greed of Sam Walton and Company in a Sunday sermon heard in several states via cable in 1992. Several important points from Barry's broadcast:

✪ What is passing for competition in America today is greed.

✪ There is a strong company in America today that owns many stores, many outlets.

✪ One of the wealthiest men in the world owns this company.

✪ He started small. You can read about it and be exuberant about the fact that someone can be broke and still make it in America.

✪ I have not liked it for a long, long time, in part because of the way I have seen little county-seat towns dry up.

✪ We are free to shop where we want to shop; that is right.

✪ But there is a lot more to it than just making money when one store, with its bigness, makes it and little stores cannot make it.

- In this mammoth organization that I happen not to be thrilled about, what he often does is not work his people long enough for the organization to pay their insurance or their hospitalization.
- They work a limited number of hours.
- They get little (or no) benefits.
- He is cutting out the middle man so he can sell to you cheaper.
- Is that really what you want, cheaper?
- Is buying cheaper the only thing that matters?
- Then you have just one big store in America and everyone else is unemployed.
- Is that what it is all about?
- I thought service was pretty important.
- I thought decency, a fair wage, and helping your employees were pretty important.
- Greed: there is a lot of difference between greed and competition.
- "Cheaper," by itself, is not enough, is it?
- This is America, and you have to take care of yourself.
- You are not even taking care of yourself when you destroy the people who were your customers.
- There are other words that ought to be spoken—rather than just, "What did you pay for it?"

Dirty Tricks-R-Us

It looks like the courts might be getting wise to Wal-Mart's unprincipled antics. According to *The Wall Street Journal*, two suppliers were awarded $7.1 million in a civil fraud case. The *Journal* reported that Wal-Mart was found to have "committed fraud by requesting under false premises that the women turn over their business records and by turning those records over to a competitor that it has already decided to hire in the first place."

RENEGE ON VENDOR CONTRACTS

The Wall Street Journal reported that in the mid-1990s the athletic-shoe maker L.A. Gear took a nasty sales hit when Wal-Mart cheaped out on a vendor contract. Wal-Mart had made an agreement to buy at least $80 million worth of merchandise from L.A. Gear. Instead, according to the *Journal*, Wal-Mart bought only about $45 million worth. Anybody willing to place bets that Wal-Mart gave the supplier a break on their agreed discount for that merchandise? Not me!

FORCE DISCOUNTS ON SUPPLIERS

As you may know, many suppliers offer a 2-percent discount if bills are paid within ten days of invoicing. According to *Forbes* magazine, Wal-Mart usually pays its bills closer to thirty days—but routinely takes a 2-percent discount even then. What's more, Wal-Mart takes the discount on the gross amount of the invoice rather than the net amount, which deducts for costs like shipping—larger amount, larger discount, and bad, bad manners from a company with the clout to throw its weight around like this.

USE A LITTLE SUBTLE INTIMIDATION

We know an executive who recently made his first visit to the buying offices of Sam's Club. There, among the unfinished plywood walls and folding tables and chairs, were signs greeting visitors that read: "How Low Can You Go?" Well, at least you know where you stand going into the interrogation, er, negotiation.

We Get Letters . . .

"I understand," writes Terrence Peterson of Nowata, Oklahoma, "that Wal-Mart not only has shafted your publisher but [many others].

"First, they buy virtually all of a small manufacturer's production, then after several months send it back . . .

"But in the meantime, the small company borrows money to produce more products—then they receive merchandise back that Wal-Mart customers have damaged, demanding *full* reimbursement for the invoiced price.

"To avoid a lawsuit, you pay Wal-Mart . . . and you're unable to borrow any more money . . . and you go belly-up."

How many times has this happened to small manufacturers who have tried to do business with Wal-Mart?

4

SIX REASONS TO BEWARE OF WAL-MART

It's no secret that I hate Wal-Mart. It's been under my skin for more than seventeen years now, and I do not love it any more than I ever have—which is not at all. Want to know another of the many things I hate about Wal-Mart? You can't trust it any more than you could trust Satan with a snow cone. Here's why.

Reason #1: Promises, Promises

Once upon a time, when Wal-Mart had just a handful of stores, Sam Walton called a managers' meeting. The wife of one manager, fearing that the chain would one day open seven days a week, was assured by Sam himself that two things were certain (no, not *those* two things):

⊛ The chain would never, ever, ever open on a Sunday.

⊛ The chain would never, ever, triple never sell alcohol, in any form.

(Remember, Sam's other never, ever rule—that he'd never, ever go into a town where Wal-Mart is not wanted? If you wonder what became of that rule, you might want to go back and look at chapter 2.)

What can Sam have been meaning to make promises like this, that he was never going to keep? Look what happened:

Retailers in the small town of Pella, Iowa, have long observed Sunday as a day of rest. Wal-Mart had been in town for nine years and seemed to respect this taboo. Then suddenly around 1990, orders came from headquarters in Bentonville: The store must open between twelve and five on Sunday. So much for the corporation's promise—and so much for sensitivity to local feelings.

But it gets worse.

Wal-Mart, by its own policy, is now universally open on Sunday, unless prohibited by a state or local law. This pretty much forces the competition to open on Sunday, too, if they want to stick around. (See sidebar, "You Will All Do It the Wal-Mart Way!" p.133) What is more, Wal-Mart employees with strong religious beliefs have been forced into an impossible dilemma: work on their Sabbath or lose their job.

According to *The Wall Street Journal*, Scott Hamby worked at Wal-Mart in Bolivar, Missouri until he was fired for refusing to work on Sunday, preferring to go to church. According to Hamby, his manager's reaction to his situation was to tell the woman in charge of setting staff schedules to "keep Scott here on Sunday until he quits." Hamby, a devout Christian and a graduate of Southwest Bible College, needed his job but cherished his convictions still more. He felt he had no recourse but to sue. A court in Springfield, Missouri, sided with Hamby.

In the wake of this lawsuit, Wal-Mart is being forced to change its policies to accommodate those who prefer to worship someone other than Sam on Sunday. *The Wall Street Journal* also notes that this settlement "could have far-reach-

Let's Keep an Eye on This One

Newspapers and TV stations down in my neck of the woods have reported that Wal-Mart is selling used merchandise as new. Steve Gardner, a former Texas assistant attorney general, asked the courts to certify his lawsuit as a class action, claiming that Wal-Mart and Toys R Us "were regularly and intentionally selling returned goods that were used, damaged, defective, or missing parts."

ing implications for other companies with weekend staffing needs that conflict with workers' religious practices."

Guess Sam met his match this time.

But what about liquor?

Oh, yes. Well, since Sam made "never, ever" promise number two ("Wal-Mart will never, ever sell alcohol, in any form"), Wal-Mart has become, by most estimates, the biggest nationwide purveyor of beer and wine.

So, two solemn pledges, two utterly broken promises. I do wish those other "dependables" (death and taxes, that is) were this easy to get around, don't you?

Reason #2: Always the Low Road

Wal-Mart got by with the slogan "Always the Lowest Price. Always" for years, until the National Advertising Review Board, which is funded by the Better Business Bureau, investigated the claim that Wal-Mart always has the low(est) price. The Board found that this just was not and is not true, and promptly ordered our pals in Bentonville to stop saying it.

Wal-Mart then had to change its motto to something that barely skipped around the law—like "Always Low Prices. Always"—so near their original slogan that the public in general still perceived that Wal-Mart had the lowest prices.

Bob Moore, publisher of the *Star-Progress* in Berryville, Arkansas (the Waltons' home turf), asked his editor and columnist, Tom Larimer, to launch an investigation. He felt free from Wal-Mart's wrath, inasmuch as the Bentonville discounter had already withdrawn advertising support from the small-town newspapers to which, in large part, the Walton family owed its earliest success in Arkansas.

Larimer described the "shopping tour" in his column, "Potpourri." Staffers came up with a list of nineteen items—from ballpoint pens to peanut butter. They divided the list in half and chose shopping days that were separated by at least two weeks, to avoid skewing the results with specials they might have encountered on only one shopping day. They picked six nearby stores—including Wal-Mart, of course—and set off to fill their shopping bags.

In the final analysis, Wal-Mart was cheapest on only *two* items—this on the first shopping day.

On the second day, Wal-Mart was the *most expensive* place to shop—and they have the register tapes to prove it.

Surveys like this one are becoming a favorite newspaper activity. After members of the Arkansas Press Association (APA) met with Wal-Mart VP of marketing, Paul Higham, (see sidebar "We don't have to explain our reasons," page 8)—and got a long-winded brush-off—they did their own informal survey.

They learned that—surprise!—prices for the same products are not the same at every Wal-Mart outlet, according to an Arkansas Press Association newsletter. If there is a Target or Kmart store nearby, that Wal-Mart's prices are forced lower.

"The bottom line: the Wal-Mart customer in a smaller community is paying more than the customer in the next town where there's a Kmart or Target."

At least one other survey—conducted by a Texas Press Association staff member in the Austin area—found Kmart's

Walton Family Values

The *San Francisco Review*, March/April 1997, tells about the second-grade schoolteacher who asked her class whether they thought a woman could be president—and only two students answered yes. This surprisingly old fashioned response prompted this teacher to design a T-shirt with the slogan "Someday a Woman Will Be President."

Somehow or other, some of these shirts got into a Wal-Mart store where they were immediately yanked from the shelves because of complaints that such a sentiment goes "against family values." Is keeping women out of politics one of your "family values?"

prices lower, on average, than Wal-Mart's or Target's for goods ranging from garden hoses to Barbie dolls.

We hope all this will motivate you to do a little price comparison on the items you purchase regularly.

Reason #3: Untruth in Advertising

Michigan's attorney general brought suit against Wal-Mart for alleged violations in the state's consumer protection act. According to *The Wall Street Journal*, Michigan's attorney general discovered that Wal-Mart's in-store advertisements were misleading: They "compared products that were not the same size or model without noting the difference, and . . . the ads sometimes inflated the prices competitors charged." Wal-Mart settled, agreeing to various changes in the way it compares its prices to those of competitors. Hey, how about honestly and accurately, for starters?

It also may interest you to know that it is "against store policy" to allow customers to jot down prices in a Wal-Mart.

It's for You

Just when you think Wal-Mart can no longer pull another one of its wool-over-your-eyes tricks, they come up with something new.

In early August 1999, Texas' Attorney General sued Wal-Mart Stores, Inc., in state court, saying its Sam's Club chain is deceptively advertising its prepaid long-distance calling cards. According to *The Wall Street Journal*, the suit filed in a Texas district court said the telephone calling cards:

- ❌ overstate the number of available minutes;
- ❌ understate the cost per minute; and
- ❌ misrepresent the savings the cards offer compared with other long-distance services.

Also according to *The Wall Street Journal,* Attorney General John Cornyn sought an injunction to stop Wal-Mart, as well as civil penalties amounting to $2,000 per violation.

That's what Virginia Berger of Spring Hill, Florida, was told when she was accosted in a Wal-Mart doing just that, according to an AP wire story. Mrs. Berger, who lives with her husband on pension and disability benefits, says she was "angry and embarrassed, and I thought they were going to throw me out." She later found no problem in writing down prices at Kmart or Target. What is the meaning of this, I wonder?

Reason #4: The Liars' Club

Another major cheek-burner for Wal-Mart's execs (as if they actually get embarrassed): In Missouri, the attorney general

Always the Highest Prescription Prices?

Don't believe all that hot air about Wal-Mart having the lowest price . . . on anything.

Take prescriptions. That's one department in which older customers might believe they can save money. But remember, Wal-Mart's "always the lowest price" is rarely, we'd guess, a reality.

We got local proof when we ran into Allan Carmena at our favorite pharmacy, Minyard's—family-owned, founded by a Dallas/Fort Worth family over fifty years ago. Mr. Carmena thought that Minyard's prices were a little too high, so he shopped "all over town" for a better deal.

Happily, he came back to Minyard's—and, before getting his prescription filled, asked with a grin: "Who do you think has the highest prescription prices in Fort Worth?"

We ventured a guess: "Wal-Mart."

Bingo!

Carmena showed the Minyard pharmacist his findings for the prescriptions that (we assumed) he and his wife take on a quarterly basis.

Wal-Mart:	$464.46
AARP mail order:	$443.10
Minyard's:	$415.76

How we'd love to post this sign in front of every Wal-Mart store in the country:

"Wal-Mart. We Make You Think We've Got Low Prices.
Always!"

blew the whistle on Walton Enterprises' misuse of the word "wholesale" in its Sam's Wholesale Club division. Folks pay $25 for an entry card to this discount nirvana. But is it a real wholesale operation? Not by the hair on my chinny-chin-chin, ruled the AG. And behold, what is this division of Wal-Mart now called? That's right: Sam's Club.

WHOLESALE, EH? NOT ACCORDING TO THE ATTORNEY GENERAL!

GUESS who we thought of when we read this quote from evangelist Frank Buchman:

"There is enough in the world for everyone's need, but not enough for everyone's greed."

Reason #5: Made in the USA? No Way

This is, I think, one of the most astounding stories I've come across in almost fifteen years of Wal-Mart jousting. This made my hair stand on end and stay that way—just because Wal-Mart is so brazen.

It starts, like so many things do, with one of Wal-Mart's creepy corporate slogans. "We buy American whenever we can" is the official line of top dogs in Bentonville, Arkansas,

It's a Bird! . . .

In Corona, California, one woman was seriously injured when a shelving unit at Wal-Mart fell and pinned her to the floor. Two others were slightly hurt in this accident and were treated at a local hospital. The husband of the seriously injured woman criticized Wal-Mart's handling of the situation: "The manager of the store didn't talk to me. I had to find out myself. They're going to have to pay the medical expenses—but all I have is a phone number." If this painfully injured lady tries to get a little money for her suffering—including medical expenses—I'll bet the Wal-Mart organization will try to fight her case all the way to the Supreme Court.

. . . It's a Plane! . . .

Wal-Mart's consuming desire to save warehouse space by stacking merchandise to the ceiling in its stores has begun to cost the discounter. I have here in my hand a clipping about a $435,000 suit Wal-Mart lost when a thirty-pound box fell on a former nurse. Her attorney presented telling evidence to the jury, saying, "25,000 cases have been filed against Wal-Mart nationwide involving customer injuries resulting from falling merchandise."

. . . It's a Motorized Ice-Fishing Augur, Falling on My Head!

"Watch Out for Falling Prices," says Wal-Mart in its TV ads. Really, you'd better watch out for falling boxes from ten-foot-high stacks of merchandise—so stacked because the company is too cheap to have adequate storage space at its stores. But after hundreds of law suits in the past ten years about falling merchandise that resulted in injuries, Wal-Mart may soon have to start making its stores safer for shoppers—particularly in Denver. That's where Phil Scharrel was injured when a forty-pound box containing a motorized ice-fishing augur fell ten feet, hitting Phil on the head and causing permanent injury.

Phil sued, as he should have, and the jury awarded Phil and his wife $3.3 million. Wal-Mart is appealing the award, of course.

Candid Camera

Here's a tale from Al Norman's *Sprawl-Busters Alert* August, 1997, issue:

A man bought a $400 camera from Wal-Mart. "I took a couple of rolls of film back there, and while looking at them, I showed the lady at the counter . . . a scratch across all the pictures, and she said it was 'a bad lens' and I should return the camera. I said, 'Great, I got it here a few weeks ago.' She said they couldn't take it back, and to return it to the Kmart down the street without the receipt, and that Kmart would give me the money . . . and for me to come back and buy a new [camera]." Is this not business ethics—and customer service—at its lowest level?

USA. And like so many of their utterings, this line makes it look like Wal-Mart is doing a good thing ("We buy American!") while offering them a way to do whatever suits them, really ("whenever we can"). Because who is to say when Wal-Mart "can" or "can't" do any old thing? Wal-Mart, of course.

So far, this is just corporate doublespeak. You and I recognize this; it doesn't surprise us; we wouldn't trust it as far as we could throw it. Now comes the sleaze.

In 1992, Wal-Mart was engaged in a heavy-duty, red-white-and-blue marketing campaign called "Buy American." Patriotic, sentimental TV commercials carried the message of an armada of Wal-Mart stores stuffed to the rafters with goods made in the USA. American flags, red, white, and blue bunting, and signs trumpeting "Made in the USA" wooed

Just So You Know

Here's what might happen if you get injured in a Wal-Mart store. Widow Phyllis Benoit went into a brand-new Wal-Mart in Westfield, Massachusetts. Mrs. Benoit slipped on a wrapped Hall's cough drop lying in the aisle, did a split (ouch!), and fractured her hip. The manager helped her get a wheelchair, and she was taken to the hospital—where hip replacement was promptly ordered. Eleven months later, Mrs. Benoit was still in pain and had medical bills of over $35,000. Wal-Mart told her attorney in no uncertain terms that the store was not responsible for her accident and would not help with medical expenses. Sad news, indeed, for a widow living on her $629 monthly Social Security check.

shoppers in every store with the same patriotic message: Wal-Mart buys U.S.-made goods; buy at Wal-Mart.

David Glass, former Wal-Mart CEO, in an interview with NBC's Brian Ross, claimed proudly that "[we] can make merchandise in this country as efficiently and as productively and for every bit the value that they can anywhere else in the world." Sounds great, doesn't it? Yet, according to *Forbes* magazine, Wal-Mart's Chinese imports coming through just one port (Long Beach) totaled 22,000 containers in 1992. This is the same year "Buy American" was at a fever pitch! Talk about a sleazy sales pitch! Wal-Mart's imports from China alone more than doubled by 1995—to 47,000 containers. A conservative estimate for 1997 put the figure at 52,000 containers—and that's just through Long Beach, which handles only 26 percent of Wal-Mart's Chinese imports.

To get a good picture of this, remember that a railroad flatcar holds two containers. When I was a kid and my Dad, a small-town railroad agent, let me take railroad car numbers for his daily reports, I learned that a flat car measured about one hundred feet long. So . . . a train long enough to haul all of Wal-Mart's 1997 Chinese imports would be 1,893 miles long, long enough to reach from Portland, Maine to Miami, Florida. And, lest you forget, the Walton empire imports from dozens of other nations too.

When Brian Ross and his NBC "Dateline" team (with their hidden camera) entered a Wal-Mart store plastered with "Buy American" signs around the mid 1990s, they found, well, a lot of foreign-made clothes. Articles made in China, Korea, Bangladesh, and Hong Kong were racked under the deceptive "Made in the USA" signs, but practically nothing actually made in the USA was to be found. These results held true in eleven stores the team visited in Florida and Georgia.

So Dateline visited David Glass in his office and presented him with a child's jacket manufactured in Bangladesh that they found racked under a "Made in the USA" sign in Wal-Mart. Mr. Glass's opinion? "That would be a mistake at the store level . . . .You'd be foolish to put a garment that said 'Made in Bangladesh' on a rack that was signed 'Made in America' and believe that you could fool people." Well, that's odd, because that seems to be just what Wal-Mart was intending with its outrageously phony "Buy American" campaign.

Apart from fooling the consumer (that's you and me, friend), Wal-Mart had a few other skeletons in its "Buy American" closet. You might want to peruse chapter 5 for more dirt in connection with Wal-Mart and its foreign manufacturing.

CHINA ... CHINA ... BANGLADESH ... KOREA
WHERE'S THE STUFF THAT'S MADE IN
AMERICA ?

Made in the U.S.A.? No Way!

Around the time of the "Dateline" story, a union local in New York state put up two $500 cash prizes (one for the union's membership, one for the general public). The goal: see who could come up with the longest list of countries from product labels in the nearby Wal-Mart. The winner came up with forty countries in sixty short minutes.

Reason #6: Santa or Scrooge?

The Walton clan is well known to be one of the two richest families in the U.S. (with estimated wealth of one hundred-billion bucks)—and equally well known for its ability to hoard its money. Yet I've noted, over the years, its absence from *Fortune* magazine's Top Fifty List of America's Most Generous (June 1999). Surely one of the five Walton family members will eventually let loose some purse strings, if for no other reason than to help fight cancer, the disease that struck down "The Master" in the early 1990s.

Not that the Waltons don't give *at all* (they know better than that). There is a Walton Family Foundation, focusing on "scholarships and assisting public school improvement." All well and good, until you study the details. In *Worth* magazine's November 23, 1999 listing of "The Benefactor 100" (which tallies lifetime giving, and doesn't count gifts to personal foundations until the money is paid out), Sam's widow, Helen R. Walton, ranks 59th, with over $68 million given to "education." But $50 million of that went to the Sam M. Walton College of Business Administration at the University of Arkansas. You'll pardon me, I'm certain, for thinking this sounds suspiciously like a boot camp for Wal-Mart's planned global takeover.

Son John T. Walton manages a *Worth* rank of 74th with his $53 million in donations. But $50 million of that will "start a scholarship program that will help inner-city and low-income children attend parochial and private schools." Wait a minute—what was that about "assisting public school improvement"?

What about corporate giving? How does Wal-Mart—the world's largest retailer, dwarfing its top five rivals combined—measure up? We're not in the business of patting the head of any of the discounters, but if such a gesture needs to be made, we'd bestow it on Dayton Hudson's Target chain for its generous giving to worthy causes. In 1999, according to our sources, Dayton Hudson averaged a million dollars a week to worthy tax-free institutions.

Let's compare Dayton Hudson with Wal-Mart. Our most recent copy of *Value Line* indicates that the Bentonville blankety-blanks (brother! . . . how we'd like to call 'em what they really are) are over four times the size of Target's parent company.

Now, let's multiply Dayton Hudson's $52 million annual charitable gifts by four. That'd be calling on Wal-Mart to give back about *$200 million* each year for the good of the people from whence it came. According to Wal-Mart's Web-based annual report for the fiscal year ending January 31, 2000, the Wal-Mart Foundation made a total of $164 million ($163,834,343, to be exact) in "Community Involvement" contributions.

Wal-Mart may be four times as big, but its generosity doesn't measure up to its competitor's. And take a look at the qualifying language in Wal-Mart's "Community Involvement Philosophy":

We also believe that being involved means more than making financial or material contributions. We strongly encourage our associates to be involved in the community by seeking out volunteer opportunities. THE MAJORITY OF OUR COMMUNITY INVOLVEMENT PROGRAMS REQUIRE OUR ASSOCIATES TO ASSIST COMMUNITY NON-PROFITS BY HELPING RAISE FUNDS. [our emphasis]

Hmmm . . . we can't help but ponder just *how much* of that $164 million comes from the volunteer efforts of Wal-Mart *associates*. Those same overworked, underpaid employees whose plight was depicted in chapter 3.

Wal-Mart is always ready to make speeches about "giving back to the community," trying to wring some publicity out of whatever tiny gestures it makes. Like the following:

EXAMPLE NUMBER ONE

When Hurricane Hugo hit Homestead, Florida, in the mid 1990s, Wal-Mart wasn't shy about making it known that it donated $1 million in goods. On the other hand, Wal-Mart was not so eager to publicize that the donation was a joint venture with some of its vendors and that the goods were delivered on Wal-Mart trucks for high visibility. When Wal-Mart was asked to name the vendors who participated, the retailer refused.

EXAMPLE NUMBER TWO

Down in my part of the country—Texas—we had a dry fall in 1998. So much so that farmers in several areas ran out of hay for their livestock.

Several Midwestern farm areas got together and contributed their surplus. Wal-Mart put two and two together and came up with a truly golden chance for publicity without having to give much of anything away.

A&E Biography on Sam Walton Reveals His True Nature

This writer, a real fan of those biographies shown regularly on the Arts & Entertainment network, was particularly interested in the December, 1997 program that spotlighted the Arkansas discounter. It gave me a chill to see how cold-blooded he really was, even with all I knew to date.

For starters, the biography said he was "the man who made small-town merchants virtually obsolete."

A&E portrayed him as a man who liked to pilot his own plane when he visited his stores. When he came into town, he liked to fly low before landing, and was frequently warned by the airport's control not to "buzz" the area. The man who wrote his biography, who rode with him several times, asked Sam what he did when he got those warnings. "I just cut off the radio," Sam said.

The segment also said that when Sam made his first big money he bought majority interest in a Bentonville state bank. And, as we understood the commentary, loaned himself money at the very lowest possible interest rate.

Sam's plan for stock options was also mentioned. Only the managers were to share in the original plan. Sam believed that only the "top guns" were in a position to help him get richer and richer. His wife, Helen, maintained that all the "workers in the trenches" should also benefit. Helen finally—the key word here is finally—shamed Sam into enlarging his stock plan.

And, finally, the A&E hour told how anti-union Sam was. Bitter. Bitter. Bitter. When one of his giant distribution centers threatened a vote to unionize, old Sam loudly said he had five hundred applicants ready to take their jobs. The threat worked.

The discounter loaded one big Wal-Mart truck with the surplus hay to send to Terrell, Texas. Newspapers were alerted. Front-page mention in several area papers. "Good old Wal-Mart to the rescue!"

All for the price of a couple of tanks of gas. Maybe one tank.

Could newspapers be the biggest idiots of all for aiding and abetting their worst enemy? (See chapter 1 to learn about how Wal-Mart pulls the plug on local advertising once it has stamped out all the competition.)

EXAMPLE NUMBER THREE

The Leesburg, Florida *Daily Commercial* patted Wal-Mart on the back for its donation of leftover Valentine candy to local elementary schools. The store's co-manager valued the gift at around $2,000, and got in this additional plug: "We contribute to the community a lot with matching grants and donations and we're happy to help again in this way."

Sweet. But a letter to the editor sounded this sour note: "This donation did not cost the retail giant one red cent. This was a charge back to the candy manufacturer . . . Wal-Mart has a standing agreement [on seasonal merchandise] with most vendors and suppliers . . . the supplier takes the loss, not Wal-Mart."

Yes, Wal-Mart takes every opportunity to tell folks it is a a good citizen. I say, take a closer look.

Since you're not doing anything at the moment, we dare you to sit down and write the following words on a postcard to:

The Walton Family
Bentonville, Arkansas

It's Good to Have Money . . .
But, Don't Let Your Money Have You

Royko Weighs In

You think I get nasty with Wal-Mart? The late Mike Royko, the nationally syndicated columnist, really dealt that crummy discounter a haymaker in his column:

Eric Mattys of St. Charles, Illinois, bought some tires for his pickup from a Sam's Club store. He was told to come back in forty-five minutes. When he came back, the man who had put the tires on was gone—and so was the truck. The man was traced and found the next day with the truck—which was stripped. He had sold the mirrors, toolbox, stereo—everything that could be sold. The pickup wouldn't run, and Eric had to pay $220 to get the shell of the thing towed home.

Back to the store he went. A manager gave him a claim number. It turns out that Wal-Mart stores are self-insured. So Eric called Bentonville. The man he talked to tried to intimidate Eric, saying the truck had been stolen by an individual and he "couldn't believe I [Eric] was trying to make a claim against Wal-Mart."

Mike ended his column with nothing but contempt for the multibillionaire members of the Walton family. "So while going to the bathroom at 3 A.M., the interest income a single Walton would earn would be enough to buy Eric a good used truck. People can be so greedy. God bless Wal-Mart," Mike concluded.

WE GET LETTERS . . .

STOP, OR WE'LL SHOOT!

Phil Bardin of Edisto Island, South Carolina, writes to warn you that if you do trade at Wal-Mart, don't buy anything without a price tag—that is, merchandise that is not price "keyed."

Phil went to Wal-Mart with a friend who bought some heavy shelving that was not keyed, so the cashier called an assistant manager to find out the price.

After much, much delay, and all merchandise paid for, Phil and friend got to the door—and triggered the alarm.

"The 'friendly' greeter asked for receipts and again scanned all the smaller bags in my companion's purse," Phil remembers. "I told him two times that it was probably the shelving. Rather than listening to me, he asked us to walk through again . . . and again, the alarm!

"By this time an audience had gathered, and you know what they thought. He checked us the third time before, finally, he was convinced that we had paid for all the purchases.

"The "authority" guy offered no apology. None," Phil writes.

On their way home, Phil and his friend estimated that they and their close kin spent an estimated $25,000 a year at Wal-Mart.

Phil recalls disappointments with many Wal-Mart purchases: the shoes he bought with clips that broke on the first day; the clothing that never lasted; the bad cuts on pictures from the photo department. He had never complained about a single one of these unsatisfactory products.

But Wal-Mart's security system . . .

"My recent encounter of being treated like a criminal is intolerable," Phil concludes.

NEVER, EVER AGAIN

I got a letter from a very unhappy (former) Wal-Mart customer from the very town where Sam Walton opened his first Wal-Mart store. Bernard I. Smith, of Rogers, Arkansas, relates:

In 1996 I switched my prescription for high blood pressure medicine from my usual pharmacy to Wal-Mart because of their advertising claiming lower prices. I picked up the prescription at the pharmacy counter, and when I returned home, I checked the prices from my old pharmacy and found that Wal-Mart was almost $3 higher than my previous supplier.

I would have accepted this as poor judgment on my part, but the Wal-Mart organization didn't think this was profitable enough so they charged me sales tax to boot. There is no sales tax on medicine.

This angered me, and I returned to the store for an explanation and a refund. They agreed to the refund plus the additional sales tax, but to collect it I was sent to the service counter. Why? I was not returning something, only trying to get back what was mine. My thought was that the refund should have come from the pharmacy register where the error was originally made.

After waiting for thirty minutes at that service counter, I vowed never to get another prescription at Wal-Mart.

Incidentally, I purchased your book and really enjoyed reading it. Couldn't agree more. Living in the heart of Wal-Mart country, I see more and more how they truly are ruining the country.

SECURITY TO AISLE 5, ON THE DOUBLE

Raul Anderson of Gainesville, Florida, tells why he quit shopping at Wal-Mart, in these colorful words:

When I go to a store, I don't feel like I gotta make a B-line straight to whatever I wanta buy—and then head right out of the store. I like to shop around and study and compare prices . . . and, just sort of 'wish' for things . . . you know, look at things I can't afford now . . . but, later, that I can get.

At Wal-Mart, though, they don't let you do that . . .

they want you to buy what you want, then get the hell out.

Every time I'd go to Wal-Mart, this was what I used to hear: 'Security scan . . . security scan . . . check down Aisle 5. Security scan . . . security scan . . . monitor Register 7.

With all that, you cannot relax in a Wal-Mart store. It's a constant barrage of security scan messages intended to make all customers feel like they are being watched. I'm even afraid to bend over and tie my shoe or try to get a better look at a product.

I'm like this: If I have done something wrong, then get me up front; just don't spoil my shopping with all those security threats.

I now go to another discount house where shopping is more dignified. So for the record, I say to screw Wal-Mart. There's more to life than low prices.

5

NINE WAYS WAL-MART IS DOWNRIGHT BAD TO THE BONE

Could I ask for a more worthy contribution to this anti–Wal-Mart book than the following excerpt from the highly respected Central Texas *United Methodist Reporter*?

Methodist Church Questions Wal-Mart's Ethics

Some 30 religious, labor, consumer, human rights and other investor groups—including United Methodist Agencies—have urged Wal-Mart to improve what they called the company's social and environmental performance.

The coalition of groups, organized by the Interfaith Center on Corporate Responsibility, said it was fearful THE COMPANY'S STRATEGIC VISION TO ACHIEVE SUCCESS IN THE MARKETPLACE COMES WITHOUT AN ETHICAL STANDARD [emphasis added].

It's heartening to hear of such organized opposition to the Bentonvillains among spiritual and social leaders.

Read through our description of nine more ways that Wal-Mart is bad through and through. Then, why not get out the phone book—or log onto the Internet—and find out which organizations are rallying to the cause in *your* neck of the woods? Bet they'd be delighted to have you help them fight the good fight.

WAY #1: Sweatshop Labor

Back in the last chapter, I promised we'd come back to all the ways Wal-Mart's "Buy American" campaign was low down and dirty and meant more than just fooling the consumer (as if that isn't bad enough).

The reality beyond the hyped-up patriotism and the downright hypocrisy of the red-white-and-blue "Made in the USA" banners in Wal-Mart's "Buy American" promotion are foreign-made goods. The labels say it all: "Made in Hong Kong," "Made in China," "Made in Korea," "Made in Bangladesh." Made anywhere overseas where we can get the cheapest cost of production, then shipped to the United States to be sold in our markets.

Labor can be bought so cheaply overseas, especially in Asia and Latin America, that retailers in the United States can often offer fantastic bargain prices on apparel and other goods and still make some money. Some would say there's nothing wrong with that: business is business. Consumers demand a good bargain, so what's a retailer to do? What's wrong, some would say, about paying only twenty-five cents of labor costs on a $19.95 pair of pants? As American union official Jeff Fiedler said in an interview with NBC, maybe Wal-Mart's slogan should be "We buy American whenever we can, except when we can get it in Bangladesh, made cheaper by kids."

In 1999, in Bangladesh's Dhaka Export Processing

Zone, workers—mainly teenage girls—were sewing shirts and pants for Wal-Mart at the Beximco factory: eighty hours a week, for nine to twenty cents an hour. Remember Kathie Lee Gifford's tears of embarrassment when she found out that clothes sold under her label at Wal-Mart were sewed by teenage and younger girls in sweatshops in New York and Central America? The news story that exposed such shameful business practices was a rare shaft of light on something all too common, despite whatever Wal-Mart's bigwigs say. Anyway, how many people believe Kathie Lee didn't know her dress line would be made in cheap-labor countries?

Charles Kernaghan, executive director of the National Labor Committee (NLC), a human rights advocacy group, testified to Congress in 1995 about conditions at the Global Fashion plant in Honduras: Thirteen- to fifteen-year-old girls were sewing those $19.95 Kathie Lee pants for Wal-Mart for thirty-one cents an hour; working seventy-five-hour workweeks, without health care. Girls were permitted to go to the bathroom only twice a day; workers were not permitted to talk to each other.

In September 1999, Kernaghan lamented, "I have a signed agreement by Kathie Lee stating that she would never again tolerate sweatshop conditions and that she would open up all shops for inspection by local religious and human rights leaders. None of these promises has been kept."

That very same month, the NLC reports, indentured workers at China's Quin Shi factory were living in penitentiary conditions, toiling twelve to fourteen hours a day, for a few cents an hour. (Even China's legal minimum wage of thirty-one cents an hour is not enough to live on.)

What were they making? Kathie Lee brand handbags that sell for $8.76 at Wal-Mart. Cheap, very cheap, by

American standards. but the sweatshop worker who makes them would have to work for more than a week to buy one.

The truth is, if you buy manufactured goods from China, Bangladesh, or a number of other countries, you can put your hands over your eyes, ears, and mouth all you like and you still won't be able to run away from the fact that at least some of those items were made by children working under appalling conditions.

There's a bizarre angle to the sweatshop story. In America, we require very little disclosure from retailers about where imported goods are made. Can you imagine shopping at your local Wal-Mart, and finding a child's sweatshirt with a tag identifying the actual Chinese factory where it was made? Impossible, you say—but an NLC shopper at a Wal-Mart Supercenter in *China* found just such a tag. China's Law of Consumers Rights requires this disclosure. It's not always followed or enforced, but at least it's on the books. In its American stores, Wal-Mart refuses to disclose the specific source of imported goods to its customers—and there's no law to make them do it.

Aside from the usual "that wasn't us, we didn't do that"-type stuff, that Wal-Mart says on the topic of sweatshops, I've managed to glean one other official comment on this deplorable issue. Lee Scott, Wal-Mart's executive vice president for merchandising at the time (who's risen to CEO in 2000), spake thus:

"The sweatshops issue is a very big, complex issue, and addressing it in a substantial way is bigger than one company or one person. I'm confident we can make some improvement, working with the rest of the industry." Spoken like a man, Lee.

The bottom line is this: Whether Wal-Mart's hundreds of overseas agents—and their big bosses back in Bentonville—

claim to know it or not, little kids are making it possible for the Waltons to be one of the richest—if not THE richest—families on earth. And by me, that stinks.

Stand and Deliver

The high-profile Kathie Lee Gifford case forced Americans to confront the reality behind cheap clothing prices. Ever since, there's been a bit more heat on the companies who make millions from the sweat of workers paid pennies a day.

In January 1999, several human rights and labor organizations filed a class-action lawsuit in the San Francisco, California Superior Court to address the plight of sweatshop workers on the Western Pacific island of Saipan, a U.S. Commonwealth. (This "technically American" status has made the island a mecca for U.S. manufacturers who want "Made in USA" products for sweatshop wages.) Among those accused, guess who: Wal-Mart!

Since then, nine companies—including Nordstrom, J. Crew, Cutter & Buck, and Gymboree—have reached a settlement. They'll require their Saipan contractors to meet strict workplace and living conditions and to stop extracting illegal recruitment fees (as high as $10,000).

But Wal-Mart, among others, dug in. They not only refused to settle—they asked the judge to dismiss the lawsuit!

On November 12, 1999, Judge Munter released his ruling: The suit has merit, and the remaining defendants must stand trial. If their conduct is found to violate California law, they could be ordered to pay back millions of dollars in past profits to provide restitution to California consumers, and to pay for a corrective advertising program.

WAY #2: "Gray Market" Merchandising

It's happened more than once: A "gray-market" product, made or imported in a way that breaks U.S. law, is found at Wal-Mart, demonstrating that, at the very least, Wal-Mart is very sloppy about checking on its suppliers' claims and warranties about their goods.

In 1993, the attorney general of the state of Florida cited Wal-Mart for selling inferior Seiko-labeled watches and falsely telling customers that the watches carried Seiko warranties. In fact, the watches had been manufactured and imported without the manufacturer's consent. When *The Wall Street Journal* called Wal-Mart about the story, a spokeswoman wouldn't comment on the allegations.

It was something like the above practice that first led me to criticize Wal-Mart in print. That was back in 1983, when I noted in *The Wall Street Journal* that Nike, the athletic shoe and apparel maker, charged Wal-Mart with trademark infringement, unfair competition, and trademark dilution. In short, Nike got ripped off. The federal suit alleged Wal-Mart was selling clothing with fake Nike trademarks. Nike sued, and won.

Nearly fourteen years later, Wal-Mart got caught doing the same thing. In 1996, a federal judge in Richmond, Virginia, found Wal-Mart and its Chinese supplier guilty of design patent infringement against . . . Nike! The codefendants, Wal-Mart and supplier Hawe Yue, had to cough up $6 million for copying and marketing Nike's Air Mada outdoor shoe. The court also issued an injunction prohibiting either co-defendant from selling any more copycat Nike shoes. But looking back to the suit in 1983, I have to wonder: do the greedy ever learn? (I do know who feels responsible: Wal-Mart officially stated that all blame and liability rests with its vendor, Hawe Yue.)

Knockoffs R Us

It's amazing how long Wal-Mart can keep fighting a lawsuit even when it knows it's as guilty as sin.

Case in point: *Tommy Hilfiger Corp. vs Wal-Mart* took five years to settle while Wal-Mart kept selling fake Hilfiger clothing and totally ignoring court orders to cease and desist. Finally, in mid-June of 1999, Wal-Mart had to pay $6.4 million to settle the lawsuit.

According to *The Wall Street Journal*, "a federal court in New York held the world's largest retailer in civil contempt twice for violating a 1996 injunction to stop selling counterfeits."

There's an ironic twist to this story. In settling the Hilfiger case, Wal-Mart agreed to donate its remaining inventory to charity. Whenever Wal-Mart gives something away, that's news, brother.

Incidentally, Wal-Mart is believed to have a standard paragraph in nearly all its foreign vendor contracts that the supplier is liable for any judgments or settlements brought jointly against them and Wal-Mart. Just another way Wal-Mart tries to avoid responsibility (and expense) at the cost of anyone, including its business partners.

WAY #3: Quota Busting

Dateline NBC, in its terrific 1992 exposé of Wal-Mart's foreign merchandising practices, uncovered one more way the retailer squeezes a few more slimy cents out of a sale: quota busting. This is a practice in which suppliers, especially in China, manufacture way more inexpensive garments than they are legally allowed to export, then sew tags in them that indicate the clothes were made elsewhere, and unload them on the U.S. market—with the help of retailers, including Wal-Mart, who are willing to turn a blind eye. U.S. customs authorities in Hong Kong say that Wal-Mart went on buying these questionable goods even after Wal-Mart's top agent in Hong Kong was warned that one of his suppliers was engaged in quota-busting.

WAY #4: Overcharging the Consumer

It's an insidious practice, and Wal-Mart isn't the only mass merchandiser guilty of it. We're talking about price-scanner mistakes. An NBC undercover team found errors on tickets at discounters, including Wal-Mart, from 10 to 25 percent of the time. And three out of four times, the error is in favor of the store! This may be due more to sloppiness than to malice, but you can bet if the ratio worked the other way (if the customer benefited 75 percent of the time), Wal-Mart and the other discounters would find a way to clean up their act.

We have a friend whose favorite sport is needling Wal-Mart checkout attendants. Long ago, Ralph (last name deleted because a Wal-Mart bouncer/security guard might threaten bodily harm) checked a register tape, found four or five overcharges, and promptly yelled loud enough to attract the store manager.

Old Ralph takes the monthly Wal-Mart sales circular to the Walton store. As he fills his cart, he checks off the items. At the check-out counter, he demands that the cashier pause after punching in each item so he can check it against the circular's sales prices.

Going on like this for twenty or so items, he takes up more cashier time than the next ten customers combined.

That particular Wal-Mart hates him more than anyone else in town. That's just what Ralph wants. He always walks out with a smile that lasts at least two days.

WAY #5: Tax Hijinks

If it weren't so darn wrong, you'd probably laugh at the ways David Glass—until recently Wal-Mart's double-tough CEO—has found to avoid or delay paying Uncle Sam his rightful share of annual revenues from Walton Enterprises.

The Wall Street Journal explains: "Mr. Glass made $9.9 million in 1998, including $1.1 million in salary, $3 million in unrestricted stock awards and $3.36 million from exercising options, according to a preliminary proxy statement filed with the Securities and Exchange Commission.

"Mr. Glass, however, deferred part of his salary so that he actually received less than $1 million in base pay, and he

Pennies from Heaven

Newsweek ran a story in October 1995 about a certain loophole the Wal-Mart family seems to have found in the federal tax code. Take a look at this one. It's a beauty.

A provision in the tax code called Corporate-Owned Life Insurance (COLI) was designed to help small businesses—mom-and-pop shops, and the like. The big-shots at Wal-Mart insure over 250,000 of the company's employees under COLI; and Wal-Mart, not the employee's kin, is the beneficiary—even if the insured is no longer a Wal-Mart employee. And the Wal is not liable for any federal taxes on the benefits.

The scheme is financed by the same insurance company that sells Wal-Mart the policies. The retailer borrows the cash to pay the premiums on COLI and borrows separately (also from the insurer) to pay the interest payments on those loans. Talk about cozy! It's a closed circle: Wal-Mart benefits, and so does the insurer; Uncle Sam and the insured worker's next of kin get nothing.

"Billionaire Heiress Faces Lawsuit Over $14,000 Bill"

The above eye-catching headline appeared on the front page of the July 23, 1999 issue of our local daily, the Fort Worth *Star-Telegram*. You can imagine how delighted we were to learn the identity of the richer-than-rich gal. Read on:

"After schlepping stuff from a posh Manhattan apartment all the way to a sprawling Texas ranch, a moving company is dragging one of the two richest American women into court. United Van Lines is suing Wal-Mart heiress Alice Walton, asserting that she stiffed the company on a $14,000-plus moving bill."

Alice, who is about $20 billion dollars rich, contends her furniture was damaged when they trucked it in last January from the two-floor apartment she quit at 39 E. 79th Street on the corner of Madison Avenue, just a block from New York's Central Park.

That apartment, for which Alice is asking $3.3 million, has a circular stairway, park views from every room, and fifteen-foot ceilings. Seven rooms. Almost 3,000 square feet.

The place she moved to in Texas ain't too shabby: the main house on this 3,200-acre ranch has a high cathedral

(continued on opposite page)

agreed to do the same for the fiscal year ending in January, 2000."

Now comes the crafty way that Wal-Mart contributes to beating up on the IRS—and all the rest of us ordinary taxpayers.

"As a result [of Wal-Mart's way of bookkeeping], Mr. Glass will receive the portion of his base salary in excess of $1 ceiling, southwestern tile and marble, and 4,432 square feet to roam around in. The property is appraised at more than $1.5 million.

If you are a Wal-Mart shopper, do think of Alice . . . and the poor moving men who may lose their jobs over a scratch or two they may (or may not) have added in handling Alice's (probably antique) furniture.

And why did Alice move to Texas?

We sent the clipping to a newspaper friend in Arkansas, with a note asking if he knew why Alice had chosen Texas for her "legal" home. His reply:

> Subject: Why Waltons Have Flown the Coop.
>
> Thanks for sending the article on Alice Walton.
> It reminded me that a number of rich Arkansans (including Don Tyson himself) have moved out of Arkansas because of our state's income tax.
> I understand that Texas does not have an income tax and that a multimillionaire (or multibillionaire, as all the Waltons are) can save considerable money by *not* living in the state responsible for providing their wealth.
> Isn't that ironic! They have billions of dollars, and can afford to live anywhere, but turn their back on their home state.

million after his retirement, allowing the company to take tax deductions on his salary; executive compensation in excess of $1 million isn't deductible, according to the Internal Revenue Service."

Puts me in mind of that old proverb that says, in essence, "The rich get richer and richer while the rest of us work like hell to pay our bills."

Wal-Mart, of course, tries to squirm out of taxes at the corporate level, too. You may recall from chapter 3 that the retailer routinely claims a discount from vendors for damage or shortage on goods received. It's up to the vendor to prove Wal-Mart wrong—and with the shipment in Wal-Mart's hands, that's well-nigh impossible. Well, the Bentonville skin-flints have tried a new twist on those shenanigans with the IRS. *USA Today* reported that Wal-Mart owes the feds nearly $32 million in taxes on losses the chain reported over four years. The problem is that, in order to write off losses due to theft, damage, or clerical errors, Wal-Mart actually has to prove the loss to the IRS; the feds want a physical count.

Nope, says Wal-Mart, we can't do it. We're too big. It's just not practical. Geez, why can't you just trust us on this one?

The last time I checked, the IRS was not buying it. It's nice, isn't it, to see that sometimes even the biggest bully on the block meets a real . . . mean . . . dog.

WAY #6: Pork-Barrel Treats

How's this for a great big glistening piece of pork? Early in 1997, *Dateline NBC* reported on a plan to build a $70 million cargo airport in Highfill, Arkansas—just fifteen miles from the Bentonville headquarters of you-know-who.

And you-know-who is footing the bulk of the bill for this international cargo port in the middle of nowhere?. That's right: you and I. Those are federal funds paying for the quick and easy import of goods made by neither you nor me. I sure hope those legislators on the appropriations committees are enjoying their campaign contributions.

Incidentally, did you know that at least as of November, 1992 (as far as we could confirm) about 15 percent of Bill and Hillary Clinton's net worth is estimated to come from Wal-Mart stock, and that Hillary Clinton served for eight years on

Oh to Be a Fly on the Wal . . .

According to *The Wall Street Journal*, "Wal-Mart's (annual) meetings stand out in part because their extravagance clashes with the penny-pinching culture of a company that sets the thermostat of each of its U.S. stores at the head office . . . .The proceedings are often less informative than hokey. At the meeting following Mr. Walton's death in 1992, an employee took the stage and pretended to converse with him in heaven. The employee said Mr. Sam wanted everybody to sing 'God Bless America.' They did."

Wal-Mart's board of directors? Yes, the mega-retailer has friends in high places: call them the First "Sam"ily, if you like.

WAY #7: Gats for Tots

As a result of a few embarrassing incidents in recent years, Wal-Mart has been forced to give up its practice of selling guns to everyone who wants one. In Fort Worth in 1992, George Lott randomly shot and killed two lawyers in a Tarrant County courtroom with a gun he bought from Wal-Mart. The Wal-Mart salesclerk had only asked him to fill out a form, but Lott neglected to mention that he was under a felony indictment. Then, in a South Texas town, a man walked up to a Wal-Mart gun counter and filled out a federal reporting form; in this case he did disclose that he'd received treatment for mental problems. Didn't matter; the clerk sold him a pistol anyway—and the man went home and killed his parents.

Wal-Mart has also gotten into trouble over a related issue. Seems Wal-Mart's in-store regulation of ammunition sales is as sloppy as its handgun efforts were. Another suit arose in

Firearms R Us

Wal-Mart got a lot of great publicity when it announced in 1993 that it would quit selling handguns in their stores. But what it didn't tell you in that semi-phony announcement was that you could still buy them from their in-store catalogs.

If you're wondering where Wal-Mart stands today in selling firearms, you'll be interested in a clipping someone sent us from a 1999 issue of *The Wall Street Journal*.

Most industry watchers believe that Wal-Mart, with its far-flung network of about 2,890 stores, is the WORLD'S LARGEST SELLER OF FIREARMS.

Only forty of its stores don't sell guns.

Iowa out of an incident in which a teenager walked into Wal-Mart, bought ammo without being asked the necessary legal questions, walked back home, and shot himself.

WAY #8: Wal-Mart: "A Bad Neighbor"?

When you are a huge rich company and all you really want is to get huger and richer, it turns out that a lot of smaller, poorer people may have to get hurt in the process. Wal-Mart, with all its size and power, could hurt people or help them in a lot of situations. Which do you think it usually chooses to do?

County surveyor Jay Poe knows. "Wal-Mart is not a very good neighbor," he told the press when a drainage problem behind Huntington (Indiana) High School originating on Wal-Mart property next door was ignored by the discounter. The problem was caused when a Wal-Mart developer commissioned the store's landscaping. The landscaper terraced

If This Story Doesn't Curl Your Toes, Nothing Will

Some Wal-Mart stories are so terrible that they make us sick to our stomachs.

Imagine a man under a restraining order going into a store—any store—and buying a shotgun without a single verbal question being asked . . . then going home and killing his twenty-two-year-old wife, the mother of his two-year-old and five-year-old daughters, and his wife's brother.

And to make this all even more sickening, this happened in 1998, a year or so after the world's largest retailer of firearms stopped selling "Saturday night specials" over the counter.

(Remember: pistols can still be had from Wal-Mart via its catalog.)

The man who did all this is serving a life sentence in prison.

The family of the young mother of course sued, and Wal-Mart has been ordered to pay the two little girls $16 million. If Wal-Mart appeals this, we hope the Alabama courts triple the award for each year the Bentonville blankety-blanks stall.

the planted green area incorrectly, and when it rained, the water seeped into the neighboring school's walls and severely damaged the tiles. "Fixing the (school's) tile is not our concern," concluded the developer. Schoolchildren's well-being is not important to Wal-Mart?

Recent events in Washington state found yet another Wal-Mart spokesman saying these same old words again: "I can assure the community that Wal-Mart wants to be a good

Snakes Alive!

A good old boy in Pleasanton, Texas reached for an automotive air filter in a Wal-Mart store and got a rattlesnake bite instead. I'll be damned if the Wal-Martians didn't claim he planted the snake there, but the fellow's attorney found that that particular Wal-Mart store had previously experienced snake problems from a nearby open field. Rather then settle this truly legitimate claim out of court, Snake Headquarters fought it in court. I'm pleased to say our hero finally received a $6,000 settlement.

neighbor." Uh-oh, what did it do now that it needs to make excuses for?

Wal-Mart secured thirty-eight acres to build a store in Central Kitsap, Washington. The site was right next to a tributary of Steel Creek, and heavy rains were due, according to local residents. Nevertheless, despite warnings, Wal-Mart, its developer, and its contractor decided to go right ahead with the earth moving to start construction.

Sure enough, the rains came, and the construction site's newly graded dirt and silt piled into the creek, wreaking untold damage on the ecosystem of salmon, eel, and grass beds. According to environmental officials, it may be years before the habitat will recover from this senseless, easily preventable devastation.

While the state's Department of Ecology levied the largest fine in the state's history against Wal-Mart ($64,000), locals think it's still not enough. "We need to ask why the company took this risk. Perhaps it didn't matter to Wal-Mart," opined an editorial in the *Central Kitsap Reporter*. I think that writer has something there, don't you?

The Nightmare Next Door

K. M. Fowler and his wife retired several years ago to build a dream home in a new housing development in their favorite town in the world—Dublin, Georgia. Thanks to Wal-Mart, their dream became a nightmare.

Soon after the Fowlers moved in, Wal-Mart contracted with a leasing company to build one of its stores on a piece of land adjacent to the Fowlers' backyard. First order of business for the contractor was to "bulldoze a long row of old oak trees along the border of their property and the subdivision—and the trees were not even on [Wal-Mart's] side of the property line," according to Mr. Fowler.

The subdivision residents protested, so the contractor built a chain-link fence.

On April 11, 1995 a windstorm "blew the fence right off the pole." Then, says Mr. Fowler, "Large quantities of trash from [Wal-Mart's] lot blew into our neighborhood. Strangers wandered into our backyards. Wal-Mart customers walked their dogs in our vegetable gardens while their spouses shopped.

"Wal-Mart refused to repair the fence, saying the property belongs to the leasing company that contracted to build the store."

Mr. Fowler even protested to the (then) president of Wal-Mart. Still no action.

After a year, the homeowners' association agreed to finance the $1,800 repair.

Mr. Fowler points out: "Part of the problem is that the Wal-Mart Corporation often does not actually own the property where it builds its stores. Instead, it signs a contract with a leasing company agreeing to become the anchor store for a new shopping complex. Thus, it effectively avoids responsibilities and obligations to the surrounding community. I hope other city councils will recognize this clever business tactic when the pros and cons of a new Wal-Mart store are being debated in their cities."

The horror of having a Wal-Mart next door—open twenty-four hours a day—continues. In March 2000, Mr. Fowler was just getting to sleep shortly past midnight when he heard "the loudest and strangest noise" coming from the Wal-Mart parking lot. Unable to sleep at 1 A.M., he got up, dressed, and drove over to investigate.

Unbelievably, at that hour of the night, workers were using a giant air hammer to break up the concrete at the store entrance! One of them told Mr. Fowler the work would be finished that night, and walked away.

Mr. Fowler went inside and found the manager on duty, who said there was nothing he could do. Why had this noisy work been scheduled for the dead of night? Wal-Mart didn't want to inconvenience paying customers at a busier time of day!

Returning home, Mr. Fowler was relieved when the noise stopped about twenty minutes later. But the noisy work continued the following night.

"At midnight," said Mr. Fowler, "it is so quiet, the noise of the air hammer sounds as though it is right outside" his home.

Check the Web page, with photos, created by Mr. Fowler's son, at www.seanet.com/~fowler/walmart. htm. Then, pronto, take Mr. Fowler's story to your city council.

Oh, No! . . . Not R.V.'s

Homeowners in the immediate area of noisy, trash-throwing Wal-Mart customers are likely to be up in arms about Wal-Mart's open-door policy—letting RVs park on their premises for up to three days at a time.

What's this? Yes, believe it or not, Wal-Mart stores welcome RV campers so that it can sell them vacation supplies and gear like fishing tackle . . . and souvenirs.

Wal-Mart even wants to sell them a customized Rand McNally road atlas that includes the address of each store and its map coordinates.

Up in Bar Harbor, Maine, Patty Rae Stanley, who owns two seaside campgrounds that charge $15 to $50 a night, is really up in arms. According to a 1999 *Wall Street Journal* piece, she is urging local politicians—and the chamber of commerce—to stop RV parking in the city limits.

"It was bad enough that Wal-Mart paved over part of town for its parking lot," she said, adding: "They've taken business from us."

Is this an isolated problem for folks cursed with a Wal-Mart store? Hardly. In Anchorage, Alaska, about ninety campers were counted on a single night.

WAY #9: A Rotten Record with Women and Minorities

Just a few items here, but I think they speak to the way things are at my favorite store to hate.

According to *The Wall Street Journal*, Wal-Mart shareholders have decided not to report publicly on the company's progress in employing more women and minorities. Many other large companies post this kind of report. What are the Wal-Mart shareholders ashamed of?

Julie Deffenbach knows. She was a jewelry department manager at a Wal-Mart in Fort Worth. She was a good employee and was singled out for praise when her department did over a million dollars in sales. Julie is also white—a fact which only becomes interesting when you learn that three of her managers, over a lunch meeting, told her she "would never move up in the company by seeing a black man," her fiancé, Truce Williams. But Julie married Truce, and about a week later, she was fired.

When Julie brought suit against Wal-Mart, the jury awarded her $119,000 in damages. Wal-Mart still denies the charge that Julie was fired over her interracial relationship and appealed the jury's decision. (How I do love to see Wal-Mart stew!)

In early 2000, I was delighted to hear that Julie Deffenbach settled, with both sides agreeing not to announce the terms of the settlement.

Four years may be a record for a Wal-Mart payoff . . .

But we did want you to know that if you are fortunate enough to get a smart, pushy attorney, it's sometimes possible to get a check from Wal-Mart before your grandchildren have grandchildren.

Wal-Mart claims it doesn't discriminate against black women. But an all-female jury in Houston thought otherwise when they awarded Angela Natt $1.4 million in damages in an August 1997 decision.

On the basis of outstanding performance reviews and regular raises, Mrs. Natt, a Wal-Mart employee since 1988, sought to move into management. Maybe she was tired of working under male managers with much less seniority than she had.

"Chainsaw Al" Has a Friend in Alice Walton

Probably the most feared man in all of the manufacturing industry is Al "Chainsaw" Dunlap.

He's the guy, you'll remember, who went into Lily-Tulip, Crown-Zellerbach, and Scott and immediately fired thousands of people. In 1996, he went into Sunbeam and did the usual: *Fortune*'s January 1997 issue says that he eliminated sixteen out of twenty-six factories and five out of six headquarters, and fired half of the twelve thousand employees. His greatest admirer, probably, is Alice Walton, daughter of Sam Walton and president of the Llama Company, one of two investment banking firms "Chainsaw Al" has called in to fund his expansion program . . . which will probably be a merger with another big company that Al can chop (chomp?) on.

Explains Alice: "The vendor base to the mass merchandisers is consolidating. The big-box guys have gotten together, and if you're too small, you don't have the ability to serve the largest retailers." Wouldn't you hate to work for somebody who thinks like Alice?—or "Chainsaw Al"?

"When she was finally promoted to manager of the automotive department of the Texas City, Texas, store in 1993, supervisors and other employees berated her with derogatory terms," according to *The Wall Street Journal*.

"She also received harassing phone calls and threats, such as a black monkey being hung over her work area," said her attorney, Eddie Krenek.

Mrs. Natt said the stress became so unbearable that she miscarried her second child, and her marriage ended. She

'Twas the Night Before Christmas . . .

Sometimes we think Wal-Mart can't possibly do anything worse to anybody than it already has. Then we read something like this in the *Fort Worth Star Telegraph*:

> A jury has ordered Wal-Mart to pay $3.2 million to a woman who said she was wrongly accused of stealing a telephone, and handcuffed in front of her children.

> The jury in rural Macon County (Alabama) returned the verdict in mid February, 1999, in favor of LaShawna Goodman of Opelika, who was arrested Christmas Eve, 1995, at the Wal-Mart in her town.

> Goodman was awarded $3 million punitive damages, which are meant to punish and deter wrong doing, and $200,000 in compensation damages.

Handcuffed in front of her children on Christmas Eve! What a helluva Christmas present for the lady's kids.

Need we add that Wal-Mart is appealing the case?

was fired two days after returning from sick leave after the miscarriage. And now the pitiful part: it took four years for Mrs. Natt to get her story before the jury.

Wal-Mart, as it's done in every case that it's lost (at least that I've heard of) is appealing. My best guess is that Wal-Mart will finally settle out of court for pennies, and I do mean pennies, on the dollar. When? Again, my best guess is that Wal-Mart's attorneys will sit on the settlement until well into this century.

An 18-Million-Dollar Apology

Should Wal-Mart be responsible for what happens in its parking lots? A Beaumont, Texas jury thinks so.

In July 1998, Donna Meissner was abducted from a Wal-Mart parking lot and raped. Meissner sued, contending that Wal-Mart "is responsible for the safety of its parking lots and could have done more to make them safer." Since then, Wal-Mart made a public apology: most unusual for Wal-Mart.

Wal-Mart eventually settled with her for an undisclosed sum. But during the "discovery" phase of the case (in which both parties are legally bound to provide each other with requested documents), Ms. Meissner's attorney, Gilbert Adams III, asked Wal-Mart to produce a study it had conducted of crime prevention in its lots. It did not. Wal-Mart attorney, Robert Rhodes, explained why in an interview: He claimed that although the retailer had indeed conducted just such a study, they were calling it a *survey*.

Talk about wide-eyed innocence! "OH—you wanted a SURVEY!! Why didn't you say so? Sure, we did a survey! But we never did a STUDY!"

Wal-Mart also failed to disclose the identity of the vice president involved in the study, as well as details of similar lawsuits against the retailer concerning sexual assault in its lots. *(continued on opposite page)*

WE GET LETTERS . . .

A SCORCHED-EARTH POLICY

One of the things I've learned since the first printing of our anti–Wal-Mart book back in May of '98 is that Wal-Mart will

According to Al Norman's Sprawl-Busters Web site, "Lawyers who bring suits against Wal-Mart refer to the company as 'an obstructionist company' because it has a track record of not producing information requested by courts during the discovery phase of a lawsuit."

This time, they didn't get away with it. The judge levied an $18 million "sanction" fine against Wal-Mart for this "discovery abuse." (Unfortunately, he never signed the order for Wal-Mart to pay the $18 million fine, so the company may avoid paying.)

Then Wal-Mart did something so shocking, you'd better make sure you're sitting down before you read on.

Wal-Mart said it's sorry.

"Wal-Mart regrets the misguided conduct that has brought us here today and apologizes to the court, to the plaintiffs, and to opposing counsel," said Ron A. Williams, the company's assistant general counsel. He added, "Wal-Mart is engaging in a searching re-evaluation of the litigation processes which have led the parties to this courtroom on this day."

There's speculation that this apology may have been stipulated in the terms of Ms. Meissner's settlement.

The judge told reporters: "I hope the stockholders do learn about this, and I hope some pressure is applied to Wal-Mart to make it behave as a responsible corporate citizen."

seemingly go to any lengths to beat any lawsuit filed against them, however just the complaint . . . like someone getting injured by objects falling from the discounter's ten foot-high shelves (see page 75). Will the Bentonvillains settle without an appeal?

Listen to this Kansas attorney:

At some point in time, Wal-Mart will have to look at its self-insurance claims departments and wonder why 98 percent goes to defend claims and 2 percent goes to the injured (I am guessing at the percentages).

In my recent dispute with Wal-Mart, I am sure $25,000 was spent by Wal-Mart to defeat a claim that could have been settled for under $10,000.

Obviously, Wal-Mart has adopted a scorched-earth policy in the hope the injured will simply give up and go away.

My client would have gotten nothing except for my determination to make Wal-Mart spend another $25,000 at a jury trial.

STRONG-ARM TACTICS

Friend Phil Bardin, co-proprietor of The Old Post Office restaurant on Edisto Island, South Carolina, sent us this eye-catching item from the Charleston, South Carolina *Post Courier*.

Donna T. Hyatt, a Union, South Carolina woman, says she was wrongly convicted of shoplifting . . . and now has the receipt to prove it.

Hyatt was accused of stealing some makeup, cigarettes, and a bathing suit, according to the police report.

Hyatt's lawyer, Harvey Breland, alleges that Wal-Mart officials arrested Hyatt to intimidate her into dropping her slip-and-fall injury case.

6

FIVE WAYS WAL-MART IS A MENACE TO AMERICA— AND THE WORLD

In a grand sense, every fact and story in this book is about some way the mega-retailer puts the screws to an America that many of us still hold damn near sacred. When

- ❂ eyesore big-box stores loom on the outskirts of small towns and Main Street becomes a ghost town;

- ❂ folks who once strolled to do their errands, visiting neighbors along the way, must drive ten miles on roads clogged with other "shopping commuters" or move; and

- ❂ cheap sweatshop goods from overseas are sold under the banner "Made in the USA,"

you could say these are all ways the Wal-Mart corporation has hurt America.

Let's acknowledge, though, that this trend is not the exclusive province of Wal-Mart. There are plenty of nationwide chains to blame for the big-box stores, fast-food outlets, and strip malls that have replaced our communities' unique local colors with the same garish logos.

But Wal-Mart is different. Scarily different. Wal-Mart's size, power, and influence on our country and our world go far beyond even the sweeping changes mentioned above.

Wal-Mart truly seems to believe it's above the law. In Bentonville, Arkansas, the grand plan has been laid out—and woe to anyone or anything that stands in the way.

"Wal-Mart is a special type of bigness," says the retail industry analyst Global Credit Services (GCS). GCS calls the Bentonvillains' dominating influence "The Wal-Mart Effect." In a report bearing that title, GCS explains the threat. Warning: This is bean-counter language, and pretty heavy sledding, but take a deep breath and read on—it's important. (All emphasis is ours.)

> . . . the disproportionate size of Wal-Mart relative to its rivals in the distribution and retailing of finished goods represents a FUNDAMENTAL IMBALANCE in the macroeconomy for the consumption of finished goods ON A GLOBAL BASIS. . . . [emphasis added]
>
> The staggering dimensions of the chasm that separates Wal-Mart from all [its] other competitors is best experienced in the form of graphs and charts. . . .

(Take our word for it—in the GCS graph, Wal-Mart's a Mt. Everest; all the rest are foothills.)

> Wal-Mart Stores is so large in scale that the low saving rate of consumers, combined with rising levels of consumer credit, must eventually lead to an increase in unfavorable conditions for a large number of retailing firms. Before most Wal-Mart shoppers give up on going to Wal-Mart for basics at daily low prices in a one-stop shopping experience, they will probably cease going to enough other stores to cause some problem at other firms.
>
> WAL-MART HAS COMPLETED ITS DOMINA-

TION OF THE U.S. Now it is time to move on to the rest of the world, and many retailing firms are waking up to this threat. [emphasis added]

Here, in more detail, are the five most frightening ways in which the world's largest retailer is casting a pall over America—and the world.

MENACE #1: Stamping Out the Free Market

We don't claim to be experts about free-market economics— you know, capitalism, consumer choice, competing products and prices, "let the marketplace decide." But "The Wal-Mart Effect" rings true. We can plainly see the country's biggest retailer becoming, in so many places, the *only* retailer in town (or several towns). We see that same retailer bent on phasing out competing manufacturers' brands and replacing them with that retailer's own private labels. Wal-Mart's overwhelming power is placing our American free market in grave danger.

Wal-Mart claims that its private-label brand goods, which now number in the hundreds, are all created to "fill a value or pricing void that, for whatever reason, the [national = other manufacturers'] brands have left behind." Thus sayeth Bob Connolly, Wal-Mart's VP of merchandising, in his best annual-report-speak—you know, that all-for-the-greater good, butter-wouldn't-melt-in-our-mouth tone.

As he goes on to explain, those mean old national brands have abandoned the poor consumer by electing to produce only "higher-end products with better profit margins." Wal-Mart to the rescue! "We want our prices to be accessible to everyone—not just a select group." Wal-Mart, defender of the downtrodden!

Wal-Mart's private labels *aren't* all more affordable. True, its Great Value products are designed to undercut those "pricey" national brands, but Wal-Mart also elbows in with its own premium-value (and premium-priced) Sam's American Choice line. When it proudly claims that all goods so labeled are grown, produced, and manufactured in the United States, we begin to wonder: Does that mean the Great Value products come from . . . somewhere else?

Here's a recent example. In August 1999, Wal-Mart introduced its own laundry detergent, in its "premium-value" Sam's American Choice line. The new soap will compete directly with the top-ranked Tide brand: a stunning turn of events for one of Wal-Mart's most loyal manufacturing friends, Procter & Gamble. Years ago, Wal-Mart teamed up with P&G, hoping to benefit from sharing inventory responsibilities and sales data with a manufacturer. P&G, eager to prove its loyalty to the ambitious Sam Walton, was perhaps the first company to open an office near the Bentonville headquarters.

So much for loyalty. Even worse, Wal-Mart is trying to ape Tide's packaging. *The Wall Street Journal* observed that Sam's detergent "is packaged in boxes and jugs whose background color is close to Tide [packaging]" . . . and "it's priced about 25 to 30 percent lower."

One nationally known marketing man put it bluntly: "Wal-Mart is really going after the family jewels with P&G."

Back to that annual report, wherein Connolly has one final word: "One of the long-term benefits of Wal-Mart's private-label expansion is that it could create strong global brands." Oh, indeed? Guess we'll all be mighty grateful in the year 2010, as we drive to our Wal-Mart to choose from among the Wal-Mart private-label brands . . . and nothing else.

Whatever line of merchandise the Bentonvillains get into

selling, they try to bully their way into becoming the number-one retailer of that industry's products. We describe elsewhere (see page 57) the ruthless tactics that made Wal-Mart the number-one seller of bicycles and outdoor power equipment—the two industries for which Quinn Publications once produced trade journals directed solely to independent dealers. Those two industries have lost almost half of their servicing dealers to the likes of Wal-Mart. The Bentonville blankety-blanks are now number one in bikes, thanks in large part to many manufacturers bowing to their every demand.

Now Wal-Mart is waving its flag as the undisputed champion in the retail toy world. In 1998, Wal-Mart's sales accounted for 17.4 percent of the market, while the giant Toys R Us dropped to 16.8 percent. Toys R Us—no angel itself in the pressure department—is gearing up for a comeback, but it may just be too late.

It's sad to see Rubbermaid drop from America's most admired corporation into "a howling mutt overnight," according to the November 23, 1998 issue of *Fortune* magazine. A company doesn't fall that far from grace without a multitude of management mistakes, but one line in the *Fortune* story was bound to catch the eye of hundreds of United States CEOs:

> Rubbermaid tried to pass along its higher costs to Wal-Mart and got a painful lesson in who jerks whose chain these days.

Wal-Mart is pursuing its competition in cyberspace with the same cunning it uses on the ground. Eyeing the boom in online book sales (as it prepared to launch its new online store: www.wal-mart.com), in July 1999, Wal-Mart announced a strategic alliance with Books-A-Million, the third largest book retail chain in the United States. Books-A-

Promote American Products! (Unless the Japanese Pay You to Do Otherwise)

During 1997, Wal-Mart turned its back on Kodak—as American a company as can be. Japan's Fuji Film Company paid Wal-Mart $200 million to take over the photo finishing operations at Wal-Mart stores, with Fuji getting extra profits from its use of its own paper and chemicals—plus preferred shelf space for Fuji film in all Wal-Mart and Sam's Club stores.

"It's stunning news in the industry," said one photo consultant. Most people in the industry expected Kodak to win this contract. It was a second loss in a short period for Kodak on the Japanese front: The American film company had also recently lost a bid for U.S. sanctions against Japan for what it claimed was Fuji's success in locking Kodak out of a big chunk of the Japanese market.

Million's massive book inventory and fulfillment system, paired with Wal-Mart's track record for ruthless domination, may spell doom for Amazon.com and its close rivals, Barnes & Noble and Borders.

MENACE #2: "The Law Is For Little People"

Pardon us for paraphrasing Leona Helmsley (you may recall the "Queen of Mean" hotel and real-estate magnate who sneered that "only little people pay taxes"). But the Bentonvillains have proven time and time again that they really do consider themselves much too big to be bothered with pesky rules and regulations.

The sad truth of it is that all too often they're right.

U.S. Mint Favors Wal-Mart in Issuing the New $1 "Gold" Coin

Have you had a tough time getting your hands on one of those year-2000 Sacagawea "gold" dollar coins? Wondering why they're so scarce? We may have the answer. Our own government played into the hands of the most ruthless discounter in our country's history.

According to *The Wall Street Journal* of February 9, 2000, "The mint crafted an agreement with Wal-Mart . . . allowing it to essentially have first dibs over most banks on the new coin."

Wal-Mart, quickly visualizing an absolutely-no-way-to-lose promotion, grabbed the opportunity and ordered **$100 million** of the dollars—virtually cornering the early market on the sure-to-be popular coins. The Wal-Mart order was thought to be the first filled, mailing the coins the very first day of release . . . while the few remaining coins were trucked to Federal Reserve banks, there to undergo a fairly lengthy count. Finally, they parceled them out to banks that were trying to meet the demands of coin collectors.

"Wal-Mart doesn't need any more advantages over a little business like mine," complained Bill Taylor, a hardware store owner in Boiling Springs, South Carolina. The American Bankers Association also protested—but to no avail.

"The U.S. Mint has done an end-run around the whole banking system," says Anne McKenna, vice president for Tiogo State Bank in Spencer, New York. "It's very disappointing."

Whether mounting an aggressive defense against the most minor customer or employee lawsuit, or denying their guilt in environmental, trade, and labor violations, Wal-Mart's lawyers are ferocious fighters. They *hate* to settle. They appeal and appeal. They drag cases out for years.

Every so often—though not often enough—the retailer comes up against a large government agency, and *loses*. Oh, how sweet it is when we get word of one of those rare victories:

Environmental regulators have taken note of Wal-Mart's heavy-handed construction activities. In February 1999, the company agreed to pay a fine of $25,000 and to perform a $75,000 community environmental project · near its Honesdale, Pennsylvania Supercenter. This settled—yes, settled!—claims made by the Pennsylvania Department of Environmental Protection (PDEP) that one of Wal-Mart's subcontractors created excess erosion and sedimentation in a nearby creek during construction of the Supercenter.

That same construction project attracted the ire of the U.S. Army Corps of Engineers, who claim the project filled in more wetland area on the site than allowed in its permit— three-quarters of an acre more. Wal-Mart is negotiating a settlement in which it would pay $200,000 to a nonprofit corporation for purchase of local wetlands conservation areas and easements.

On August 23, 1999, the Federal Aviation Administration (FAA) proposed a $50,000 civil penalty against Wal-Mart for allegedly violating hazardous materials regulations—shipping hazardous materials without the proper packaging and inadequately labeling them. The retailer had thirty days to respond to the allegations.

The FAA alleges that Wal-Mart improperly offered a shipment containing dry-chemical fire extinguishers for transport by Airborne Freight Corp. from a facility in Hermiston,

Same Theme, Different Country

From *USA Today*: "Wal-Mart's 4.7-acre Supercenter in Mexico City was (recently) closed for a day because of import violations. Two Mexican newspapers reported that 13,707 products in Wal-Mart's inventory didn't comply with import-labeling rules." Shame, shame, you low-down Bentonvillians.

Oregon, to Seymour, Indiana. The extinguishers were neither packaged properly nor labeled as required by the Transportation Department, according to Elizabeth Isham Cory, FAA spokesperson.

Employees at the sorting facility noticed stains on the outside of a container. One of the fire extinguishers didn't have a pin, and about half a pound of hazardous material had leaked out.

The FAA had increased its number of hazardous-materials inspectors since 110 people were killed in the May 1996 crash of a Valujet airliner in the Everglades—a crash attributed to oxygen generators mislabeled as empty, which caused an in-flight fire. Unbelievable, isn't it, that Wal-Mart thought it could ignore a federal regulation so soon after a notorious violation with such tragic consequences?

The biggest Wal-Mart environmental-violation case we know of involves water pollution in three states, with penalties calculated at $5.6 million. The U.S. Environmental Protection Agency (EPA) wants to bring suit against Wal-Mart and five of its contractors, alleging they violated terms of their 1992 storm water permit for developments in Texas, New Mexico, and Oklahoma.

"The $5.6 million maximum fine is 'very large' compared with other EPA enforcements in the region," EPA spokesman Dave Barry said.

Fining the maximum seems to indicate that Wal-Mart and its contractors are guiltier than nine kinds of hell of polluting thousands of acres of land and countless numbers of streams.

A Wal-Mart spokesman said, with a perfectly straight face, "It's the first time Wal-Mart has been cited by the EPA." We hate to call anybody a fibber, but we seem to remember Wal-Mart being caught on a similar storm water charge in Washington state a few years ago, and paying a huge fine for the polluted flow that killed tens of thousands of salmon and other fish. And a quick check of EPA records on the Internet shows an Administrative Order filed in December 1996 against Wal-Mart (no details are given), and, in 1997, a "Notice of Proposed Administrative Penalty Assessments and Opportunity to Comment." The EPA proposed to assess an administrative penalty of $125,000 against Wal-Mart and CRAIG General Contractors of Bedford, Texas, for their failure to implement a complete Storm Water Pollution Prevention Plan (SWPPP), and for operating a construction site in violation of their National Pollutant Discharge Elimination System (NPDES) permits.

MENACE #3: Supercenter Consolidation

In the first edition, we sounded a warning about Wal-Mart's new Big Thing, the Supercenter: a megastore offering not only the whole range of goods that the old-style Wal-Mart might contain, but also such things as a supermarket, an auto service depot, a bank branch, a shoe repair shop, a video rental shop, a pharmacy, a restaurant (such as McDonald's)— just about every segment of a typical town's small business commerce that the original Wal-Marts hadn't previously driven out of business.

Even worse, when the retailer brings in a Supercenter, it often "consolidates"—systematically shutting down one, two, or three original Wal-Mart stores nearby and thus forcing all its customers to drive even farther to the "new, better, bigger, shinier" Wal-Mart Supercenter.

This invasion continues, of course, but now with more emphasis on consolidation. Since it has reached market saturation in many of the regions where it started, mainly the south and the Midwest, the retailer's sales growth at those stores is slowing. With much of its competition stamped out, Wal-Mart has "maxed out" its market share, of the goods and services that a typical Wal-Mart supplies, that is.

Shutting down stores and forcing customers to drive farther to a Supercenter (cheaper for Wal-Mart than running several stores) is one solution. Reaching into urban outskirts and other resistant pockets of America with Neighborhood Markets is another—for more on that, read Menace #4.

CASE STUDY OF "RELOCATING": HEARNE, TEXAS

If you think I've been saying some harsh things about Wal-Mart, you should listen to what the people of Hearne, Texas, thought of Sam Walton's family company.

A Wal-Mart store moved into the outskirts of Hearne in, or about, 1980. From that point on, one by one, virtually all the major stores on Main Street closed, and Wal-Mart became the main game in town. Now, one would think that with half of the town's business coming its way, Hearne's Wal-Mart would have become a permanent, prosperous fixture.

Hardly. With the Texas economy slipping, Hearne's Wal-Mart dropped from 115 employees to ninety.

Then came a bombshell. In 1990, the Bentonville, Arkansas–based discounter announced it would be closing the store, claiming the company had been losing money all the ten years it had been in the area, which just has to be 100 percent baloney. What happened, of course, was that Wal-Mart opened some much larger stores in nearby cities that enabled it to close its lesser dollar-volume outlets.

So, said Wal-Mart in essence, to hell with Hearne.

Listen up to how some Hearne residents expressed their feelings:

❂ Archer Hoyt, a drugstore owner was bitter, bitter. "When he (Walton) came in, the whole pretense was 'I'm for Little Town America and I'm going to give you some of the benefits that big cities have.' Now that he's gotten the cream of the crop out of the county, he ups and leaves."

❂ Dave Cunningham, president of the Hearne Chamber of Commerce, doubted Wal-Mart's claim that the local store lost money for the ten years it was in Hearne. Cunningham felt Wal-Mart's closing puts something of a stigma on the community. He said that if the store had closed after the first year, "We'd still have a vital downtown."

❂ Burt Lockhart, who runs a store his father opened thirty years ago, said, "They breeze into town and suck up all the business, then once all the businesses are gone, they pick up and leave."

❂ Salesclerk Kathy Jackson, 32, said she worked up to thirty hours a week to support herself and her father. Ms. Jackson earned barely above minimum wage with no benefits. "I really haven't made up my mind [on what to do]. The reality of it hasn't hit."

❂ Dawn Hintzel, a legal secretary and a customer of Wal-Mart said, "It makes me very angry to think they could walk into Hearne ten years ago, set up shop, drive all the other retail business out, and then turn around and leave us holding the bag."

What has happened to the town since Wal-Mart packed up and left?

I talked to druggist Archer Hoyt, who inherited his drugstore from his father and grandfather. Archer had a beautiful success story, with an expanding store—until Wal-Mart opened a prescription pharmacy at its Hearne location.

Archer fought back with lower prices on everything, but the profits shrank, almost to nothing. Archer then started advertising strongly on his delivery service, which Wal-Mart couldn't furnish, and started offering thirty-day credit terms to his older customers. Finally, Archer gained back about a third of the business he lost, but it has been flat from that point on. Eventually he had to close, and is now working for a Texas-based chain of supermarkets that have pharmacies.

The rest of the Hearne merchants probably fared worse than Archer. Much of the downtown is boarded up—and likely to stay that way. The young people who might have taken over if there had never been a Wal-Mart have moved on to the cities. Anyway, who wants to open a store in Hearne when much of the town is now driving to the new Wal-Mart Supercenter in nearby College Station?

"Now, believe it or not," Archer lamented, "you can't even buy a white shirt—or even underwear—in this town that once had several thriving dry goods stores."

Bottom line on the Hearne story: Over a ten-year period, the town lost so many of its merchants that Wal-Mart was the only source in town for scores of essential, everyday items. Wal Mart had made Hearne into a crippled town then booted its crutches out from under it.

SUPERCENTERS SQUEEZE OUT THE SMALL TOWNS

The way to kick up the amount of sales per square foot is to offer more goods and services in a single location, so that location (the Wal-Mart Supercenter) comes away with a larger share of the consumer's dollar. Supercenters are more efficient than the standard-issue Wal-Mart store; that is, when a customer leaves a Wal-Mart Supercenter, that customer takes home fewer consumer dollars than when leaving a typical Wal-Mart, because he or she has also done the grocery shopping, the banking, prescription drug and eyeglass purchases, car maintenance, and any number of other errands right there in the Supercenter.

This is all just cherry pie for Wal-Mart, but think about the way the landscape is starting to look for poor us in small-town America: Every fifty miles or so a great big shiny does-it-all Wal-Mart, and nothing, nothing, NOTHING in between. Where is competitive pricing going to be then, I wonder, when there are no competitors around? This nightmare vision is extreme, granted, but it's Wal-Mart's most cherished dream. Bank on it.

MENACE # 4: First the Supercenter, Now the "Neighborhood Market"

Shutting down superstores and forcing customers to drive farther to a Supercenter is a menacing strategy that's devastated our more rural areas. Reaching into urban outskirts and other resistant pockets of America with Neighborhood Markets is another.

As of January 31, 2000, there were 721 Supercenters in the U.S.—with 165 more in the works—and 383 more around the globe. Now comes a devilishly ingenious new approach: the Wal-Mart "Neighborhood Market." Sounds cozy, no? So what is it? Well, it sounds a lot like your mom-and-pop market—on steroids. And like the mom-and-pop, the new "small" Wal-Mart outlet is mainly a grocery store, with one third devoted to general discount merchandise, plus a drive-through pharmacy. But "small" is relative—the Neighborhood Market averages forty thousand square feet and covers about as much acreage as a football field.

What's the strategy behind these "mini Wal-Marts"? In the 1999 annual report, then-CEO, David Glass, remarked, "We think there may be some business that we are not getting purely because they may not be as close to the customer or convenient for small shopping trips. That's where we think there may be an opportunity for the small grocery/drug store format . . ."

Since a proposed new Neighborhood Market will take up "only" one-half to one-quarter the acreage of a monster Supercenter, Wal-Mart may be more likely to sneak it in "under the radar" of an unsuspecting town—or even a fiercely anti–Wal-Mart town. Al Norman's Sprawl-Busters Web site describes how residents of Plano, Texas fought off a planned 113,000-square-foot Supercenter . . . so Wal-Mart came back with a 52,000-square-foot Neighborhood Market. Caught off-guard, exhausted from a long struggle, the folks of Plano may not regroup fast enough to fend off the new threat.

The Neighborhood Markets are Wal-Mart's newest "merchandising laboratories." And who can fault them for trying to detect what customers want, and deliver it? Well, for starters, the owners of thousands of honest-to-goodness *neighborhood markets* across the country, still serving their neighbors, who will be driven out of business by the latest weapon in the Wal-Mart arsenal.

The Small Grocery Store . . . Going . . . Going . . . Gone

One by one, the mom-and-pop grocery stores that were once the backbone of small-town America are disappearing. The Food Market Institute says their numbers dropped **40 percent** between 1988 and 1998.

In February, 2000, Associated Press feature writer, Josh Hoffner, visited Dennis and Pam Hatzenbuhler of D & P Foods, the only grocery store in Flasher, North Dakota, serving this community of three hundred people for the last seventeen years.

"We're fighting tooth and nail to stay around," says Dennis. But with the likes of Wal-Mart choking out mom-and-pop stores, how long can they survive?

The problem now is getting suppliers who can justify "coming out this far"—to off-the-beaten-path retailers. And, how can a small grocery compete with the Wal-Marts who buy by the trainload rather than the single carton?

The Wal-Marts of the world are also able to add to their profit percentages by charging big food and beverage makers for eye-level space at the end of the aisle, thus allowing these monster stores to sell at discount prices.

Ernie Hinder of Flasher was close to tears as he told the AP writer, "We'd be plumb lost without a grocer here."

Hatzenbuhler concludes, "The grocery business used to be a fun business, but now it's a stressful business. Customer loyalty is a thing of the past."

Maybe the Hatzenbuhlers can get a job at Wal-Mart . . . at near-poverty wages.

MENACE #5: International Expansion

The United States has only 4.5 percent of the world's population, so the way we see it, that leaves most of the world as potential customers.

—Bob L. Martin, president and
CEO of Wal-Mart International

Everybody's Home Town Store
—Wal-Mart 1999 *Annual Report*

Just think of all the people in the world who haven't had the opportunity to shop at Wal-Mart.
—David Glass, president and CEO of Wal-Mart
Back cover, Wal-Mart 1999 *Annual Report*
(below the headline: "A world of opportunity,"
and a huge Wal-Mart "Smiley Face"
imposed on a yellow Earth)

Wal-Mart's drive for global domination, still in its early days when we warned you about it in our first edition, has since taken on real—and really terrifying—dimensions.

I've got copies of Wal-Mart's fiscal 1999 and 2000 annual reports in hand, and they make my blood run cold. (Ever read one of these things? Scaaaarrry stuff! You wonder if the folks who are writing this actually believe themselves, or if they just close their eyes and think of England, or whatever, the whole time.)

Wal-Mart cheerfully lays out what's in store for America and the world—the gospel according to Bentonville. Let's focus on the special "International" sections of the 1999 and 2000 annual reports.

The fledgling international division had its first profitable year in fiscal 1997. Then-CEO David Glass's 1998 estimate of Wal-Mart's international sales growth: *perhaps*, in *five*

German Government Stands Up to Wal-Mart

Wal-Mart might finally have met a government that won't tolerate its despicable strong-arm sure-fire way of stomping its competition—selling have-to-have products below cost. Just before this book was off to press, our hometown newspaper reported that the German government "ordered the U.S. giant and two German rivals to call off their price war on groceries—because it could drive mom and pop shops out of business . . . Wal-Mart [was] selling staples . . . below cost on a regular basis, a practice that is illegal in the highly regulated world of German retailing."

Maybe our government should consider doing something to help America's small grocery stores.

years, they might account for 10 percent of the company's total sales.

Now let's flash forward just *two* years: for fiscal year 2000, international sales made up over **13 percent** of Wal-Mart's $165 billion total sales. Taken all by themselves, international sales rose **63 percent** in fiscal 1999, and profits, **110 percent.**

Wal-Mart's now the **largest retailer in Canada** (with 35 percent of the discount-and-department-store retail market). And the **largest retailer in Mexico**.

By 1999, Wal-Mart's foreign outlets had grown from **300** to **715.** The 2000 annual report, headlined "Banner Year for International Expansion," announced a new total of **1,004** foreign outlets. A figure boosted, in large part, by the purchase of the German chains Wertkauf (twenty-one stores) and Interspar (seventy-four "hypermarts"), and the British retail chain ASDA, with its 229 stores.

ASDA, it turns out, has been cheerfully imitating the

You Will All Do It the Wal-Mart Way!

We *told* you they're out to dominate the globe. Having learned how to force its competitors into matching Wal-Mart's business hours, the discounter's showing those stodgy old Europeans the error of their ways. It's all in the 2000 annual report, and we just couldn't do a better job of describing this new world order:

> Wal-Mart has already made a major change in the shopping culture of Germany simply by opening [its] stores two hours earlier than the 9 A.M. standard. German laws allow shopping to begin at 7 A.M., but most shops in the country wait at least two more hours to open.

Anyone want to bet how long it will be before the German shopkeepers are forced to start setting back their alarm clocks two hours?

"But wait," you say, "the Germans are a proud people; they stick to their traditions!" Think so? Read on—and shudder . . .

Germans seem to enjoy browsing the stores when crowds are smaller. Though they were initially alarmed to find greeters talking to them when they entered the stores, the friendly, smiley-faced Wal-Mart culture has now established a firm foothold.

Wal-Mart "culture" for years. You know: grinning greeters at the door, "permanently low prices forever," coining its own smarmy title for employees (not "associates"; they're all "colleagues"); even, I swear, yellow Smiley faces. But then, ASDA's stock-in-trade is "borrowing shamelessly" the ideas and practices of other companies.

The Wal-Marts Are Coming!
The Wal-Marts Are Coming!

We tried to warn them, but it was probably too late . . .

On Thursday, June 17, 1999, two London newspapers contacted the author. Probable reason: Wal-Mart had bought the British retailer ASDA and would soon be arriving on their shores, bringing The Wal-Mart Way to merrie olde England. And this book of ours seemed to be the only one in the bookstores that's 101 percent pure anti–Wal-Mart.

First call: a thirty minute interview with a *London Telegraph* reporter whose questions pretty much centered around what Wal-Mart's competitors and vendors could expect when Wal-Mart begins operations in England. We painted the worst possible picture. The story, about eight hundred words, appeared in the following Sunday's *Telegraph*.

Next call: *London Sunday Mail* business editor Russ Hotten, asking if we'd be interested in writing a one thousand-word story on Wal-Mart's forthcoming invasion. The *Mail* would pay $1 a word. (That's $280 *more* than we made in our very first year of newspapering.)

"Our"*Mail* story appeared the following Sunday (June 20, 1999). We could go on and on about their rewrite . . . but the headline was a grabber:

Ruthless retailer "has killed a way of life"
—and the details were there. We laid it all out: the lost jobs, the squashed vendors, the scorched earth in Wal-Mart's wake.

Too late to stop the ASDA purchase. Perhaps not too late for our British cousins to arm themselves against the invasion from their former colony.

Oh, Canada . . .

Soon after Wal-Mart bought Canada's Woolco chain, the retailer had "already stepped on some cultural sensibilities," according to *The Wall Street Journal*. A Montreal newspaper reported that Wal-Mart was requiring "750 managerial personnel . . . to log an extra twelve hours a week without a salary increase."

Wal-Mart "is the model of savage capitalism," growled the president of a Quebec foundation.

"The businesses are so similar that it's almost spooky," enthuses Allan Leighton, CEO of ASDA and president of Wal-Mart's UK operations.

Spooky? Mr. Leighton, you took the word right out of my mouth.

When the British press reported the ASDA purchase, it seems that most of them just rolled over and reprinted Wal-Mart's press-release blarney about what a great asset it'd make to the British Isles. The Sunday, June 20, 1999 *London Financial Mail* enthused that "Wal-Mart clearly has many fans in the U.S. because in a recent major survey the company was voted Number One Corporate Citizen of America for its community commitment."

We still haven't been able to trace the origin of this honor. *Fortune* magazine does list Wal-Mart number *five* in its top ten list for the "Most Admired Companies." Chosen how, you ask? Well, *Fortune* has Clark Martire & Bartolomeo (CM&B) poll 10,000 executives, directors, and securities analysts. We can see why those folks would kowtow to the world's biggest retailer. But we note that Wal-Mart doesn't make it onto *Fortune*'s list of the "100 Best Companies to

"Never resist change . . . We have to be able to place a store or club side-by-side with the competition and beat them every time."

—David Glass
Director and Chairman of the Board, Wal-Mart
2000 *Annual Report*

"Resistance is futile. You will be assimilated."

—The Borg
"Star Trek" series

Capitalist Pigs

In spring 2000, as a bill to grant China permanent normal trade relations passed the U.S. House and moved on to the Senate, we thought of human-rights activist Harry Wu and his impassioned campaign to raise consumer awareness about the horror behind cheap Chinese imports. Wu, who was imprisoned for nineteen years in a Chinese labor camp and has been imprisoned there for protesting the Communist regime's policies, has led rallies at Wal-Mart stores in Auburn, Washington, and Las Vegas, Nevada, protesting the retailer's sale of products made in China. According to the Las Vegas *Sun*, Mr. Wu alleges that Wal-Mart has bought products **directly from Chinese military companies**. At the Las Vegas rally, Wu showed a pair of Wal-Mart binoculars he said were made by Norinco, a Chinese company with military ties, according to the *Sun* article. Norinco had allegedly been caught smuggling AK-47s to American street gangs, the *Sun* reports.

"Cheap products mean cheap labor," said Wu. "Cheap labor means cheap life, which means the abuse of human rights."

Work For"—those results are based two-thirds on *employee* surveys, and one-third on the companies' claims.

But back to ASDA. Until Wal-Mart acquired it, that chain was the third largest retailer in the United Kingdom. Since then, ASDA's been price-cutting "in a bold move to build market share." We can only hope and pray that Britain's other retailers have opened their eyes and ears to the frantic warnings from the anti–Wal-Martians across the Atlantic.

If they just read the 2000 annual report, they'll find the danger spelled out in remarks like Allan Leighton's:

> There are a group of competitors who take the attitude that 'this too will pass,' and [they] will probably not survive.

7

HERE'S WHAT YOU CAN DO ABOUT IT!

You've had an earful of the lowlife things Wal-Mart and the Walton family have pulled on you to make the Waltons almost **100 BILLION DOLLARS RICH**. That's more than the GNP of the vast majority of the third-world countries; more than the net worth of the entire Rockefeller family—heirs of Standard Oil, a company the U.S. government called a monopoly more than three-quarters of a century ago.

Is Wal-Mart a monopoly today? Without a doubt, it has monopolized the consumer dollars of small-town America, through its buying power, underhanded marketing, and callous disregard for paying its proportionate share toward the growth of the communities in which it flourishes. But a monopoly? In its report "Wal-Mart 2000," the retail industry analyst Global Credit Services (GCS) takes the following view:

> [D]on't even think that Wal-Mart is the next Microsoft, because this is not a monopoly in any sense of that word. Wal-Mart is merely the most amazing development in retailing since Sears, Roebuck decades ago during the 20th century . . . [and] in the 21st century . . . the phenomenon among all wonders of the world of retailing.

The report goes on to explain that Wal-Mart is huge, alright, but it still has competition—chiefly from the "Big Five" of Sears, J. C. Penney, Home Depot, Kmart, and Target. Not exactly knights in shining armor, but, OK, competition.

Then GCS stacks up the Big Five's **combined** sales over the past four years and compares it to Wal-Mart's:

TOTAL SALES, 1996–1999

Big Five (combined total)	$630,584,000,000
Wal-Mart (alone)	$525,464,000,000

GCS projects that Wal-Mart should match the combined sales of the Big Five, with ease, by the end of the year 2000. Even worse:

INCREASE IN SALES FROM 1996 TO 1999

Big Five (combined total)	34 %
Wal-Mart (alone)	57 %

It's a pretty gloomy picture, but before we fold up our tents and go home, remember that Wal-Mart has yet to conquer America's biggest cities. There's just too much choice there, too much competition for even a Wal-Mart to swoop in and pick off. And it's in those urban centers, too, that the dedicated grocery chains such as Safeway, Albertson's, and Kroger—staffed by unionized workers—still hold their ground.

They know they're engaged in the fight of their lives. Even without America's cities, Wal-Mart and Sam's Club combined already rank as the **world's largest supermarket operator**. The "Neighborhood Market experiment" is Wal-Mart's driving wedge to penetrate the urban stronghold. Still, judging from the union victory we celebrated in chapter

3, the grocery chains have a chance to hold the line with Wal-Mart (if not turn the tide).

You can join the fight. Whether you're a retailer competing with Sam and Company, a supplier selling to them, an "associate" struggling to get a fair deal, a citizen concerned about Wal-Mart coming to town, or a consumer looking to your own bottom line and the well-being of your community, we're here to help you gain the satisfaction of a battle well-waged in your dealings with Wal-Mart. We'll start with five general approaches anyone could use, then detail a couple of dozen specific tactics for retailers, suppliers, citizens and planning boards, or consumers to try.

Can We Keep Wal-Mart Out of Our Cities?

In the last few years Wal-Mart has begun nibbling away at the small, incorporated cities that surround the big urban centers. Few bothered to fight back, because they wanted the 1-percent state sales tax that Wal-Mart would divert into their coffers from the big brother city.

But now the Walton family wants to get its giant 200,000-plus square foot Supercenters into the big cities—not just one store per city, but several locations that will siphon off grocery business from the grocery chains (which, with all their faults, are better citizens by far than the Walton family).

How to block the blankety-blanks?

First and foremost, it takes some legal work—from an attorney skilled in working with municipalities. As we understand it, a city's zoning and planning commissions can put up a lot of high hurdles for Wal-Mart to jump before they become the merchant of death to the independent business-people who are the backbone of your city.

One place that was able to keep Wal-Mart out was Lake Placid, New York, the town that hosted the Winter Olympics in 1980. Keeping Wal-Mart out cost the town and the Adirondack Park Agency less than $70,000. The *Lake Placid News* quoted Wal-Mart attorney Tom Vlesewicz as saying "Wal-Mart has already spent over $5 million on the Lake Placid project." Quite a victory, considering the town was hugely outspent . . . in a fight that lasted five years.

If your town or city is threatened by a new Wal-Mart or one of its all-consuming Supercenters, you might want to write the *Lake Placid News* asking who to contact there should you want to send your anti–Wal-Mart council a step-by-step fight plan. You'll find more, below, in the suggestions for "Citizens and Planning Boards."

Write Your Local Newspaper

Do the local newspapers and banks share any responsibility for helping Wal-Mart kill off their small towns? We'd have to answer a qualified "yes." (And add, they may offer a couple of smart ways to keep Wal-Mart's mighty paws off *your* town.)

Let's talk about the small-town newspaper first. Years ago, Wal-Mart did do some advertising in local papers—knowing later they'd have a few favors to ask in return:

✪ Front-page attention if Sam himself came by to inspect the store.

✪ Front-page mention if the local store awarded one of its $1,000 scholarships to a graduate.

✪ Picture and a story if a new manager came to town.

✪ Picture and a story when an employee was recognized.

And so on—you get the picture.

Then, all Wal-Mart support of weekly newspapers stopped. The Bentonville headquarters ruled that the only advertising would be a monthly circular of specials via the postal service.

But the Wal-Mart manager continued to call the papers for publicity. Then—right then—the editor should have told the manager where to go. But very few editors did that.

Today, when subscription money is totally necessary to keep the paper afloat, the publisher is not likely to editorialize against Wal-Mart, for fear that you might cancel your subscription—and people do cancel on the slightest provocation.

But the paper *will* run your anti–Wal-Mart letter. Certainly, every merchant it's put out of business should write a letter any time and every time Wal-Mart does *anything* they don't like. For instance: for not supporting your local hospital's drive for money . . . or not pitching in its part for helping to pay for band uniforms . . . or football and basketball uniforms . . . or for a donation on a project your local Chamber of Commerce wants for your town. The possible grievances are as endless as Wal-Mart's pecuniary ways.

And you can bet your newspaper publisher will run that letter . . . for the good of your town . . . and for his own good in getting back at the blankety-blanks that baited him with a few ads when the store came to town . . . then pulled the rug out from under him.

Write that letter!

Enlist Your Hometown Bank

You should also feel sorry for the home-owned bank where you might be depositing your hard-earned money. They also got suckered when Wal-Mart came to your town. They might have believed that Wal-Mart would become a major depositor.

Not so. The bank's only gain is the measly fee they charge for taking the store's cash receipts via the drop-through night deposit box and wiring out the money the following morning to Wal-Mart headquarters in Bentonville, Arkansas—not leaving it long enough to "dust the floors," to borrow a phrase from the *New York Times*' depiction of how little independent banks benefit from a Walton Enterprises outlet.

And about those one hundred new jobs Wal-Mart might bring to town? Well, for every one hundred jobs Wal-Mart brings in, more than 150 jobs are lost in the area that particular Wal-Mart store serves. We should add that about 75 percent of those "new" Wal-Martians will be paid so little, it's doubtful the bank would get more than a single handful of new depositors.

While we're on the subject of banking, the worst has been narrowly averted, at least for the time being.

In 1999, Wal-Mart was primed for a sneaky entry into the savings bank business. That's right, they wanted you to get all your *banking* done at Wal-Mart too! What was Wal-Mart's foot in the door? The "mere" acquisition of a one-branch savings bank in Broken Arrow, Oklahoma.

But in July 1999 an organization called the Inner City Press/Community on the Move & Inner City Public Interest Law Center (based in the Bronx, New York) filed a challenge with the Office of Thrift Supervision, filled with convincing arguments against letting the Wal-Mart fox into the banking chicken coop.

This filing—followed by last-minute revisions to a piece of financial modernization legislation signed by President Clinton in November—effectively killed off Wal-Mart's bid to enter the banking industry (and to eventually, you can bet, stamp out whatever's left of the hometown American bank).

Will Wal-Mart keep trying? Do chickens have lips?

Bottom line: If and when you want to start a "crusade"

to keep Wal-Mart from expanding its local (non-grocery) out-let into a Supercenter (100,000 square feet or more), try en-listing the president or chair of your bank to lead the drive. They should be well aware that their industry just squeaked out of Wal-Mart's clutches.

Who You Gonna Call?

Sprawl-Busters! So far as we know, Al Norman is the number-one specialist in keeping a Wal-Mart from coming to your area—or keeping the Wal-Mart you have from expanding into a Supercenter.

Al is a former newspaperman who has dedicated himself to keeping Wal-Mart in particular—and superstores in gen-eral—from consuming Retailing America. His web site www.sprawl-busters.com, with its News Flashes from the front lines and Sprawl-Busting Victories, is a real shot in the arm for anyone who thinks that the fight's been lost. Don't you be-lieve it!

Al's book, *Slam Dunking Wal-Mart!—How You Can Stop Superstore Sprawl in Your Hometown*, should be on every Wal-Mart hater's coffee table. We've read it. Liked it. Well worth the money. You can order it from his web site (see above).

Quite a few towns and cities have called Al Norman for on-site consultation. You should too if you're even remotely expecting Wal-Mart to put up a nasty fight in bullying them-selves into your town or city..

Fight 'em in Cyberspace!

If you've got Internet access at work, at home, or at the li-brary, you've got a direct line to an amazing wealth of infor-mation, from horror stories to organized opposition. Check out these anti–Wal-Mart web sites (and Wal-Mart's own sites):

✪ **www.walmartyrs.com** "Sharing the Wal-Mart Experience Worker-to-Worker," this site is produced by the United Food and Commercial Workers International Union (UFCW), which is engaged in several ongoing legal battles surrounding Wal-Mart meat-department workers' efforts to unionize. Plenty of workers' horror stories and information about workers' rights.

✪ **www.walmartwatch.com** Also produced by the UFCW, this site focuses on the impact of Wal-Mart on consumers and towns. Unfortunately, the site's wealth of statistics, anecdotes, and news items are all undated.

✪ **www.wal-martlitigation.com** The home page of the Wal-Mart Litigation Project, which gathers, refines, and markets information about lawsuits against Wal-Mart. Coordinated by Nashville, Tennessee attorney Lewis L. Laska, the project aims to "assist lawyers who sue Wal-Mart to force the company to act properly toward its customers and employees . . . to 'level the playing field' so plaintiffs have a better chance of winning suits where Wal-Mart has done wrong."

The Wal-Mart Litigation Project sells packets of information on types of cases (such as customer injury, shoplifting disputes, wrongful termination), verdicts, and settlements. The project also lists lawyers willing to take on a suit against Wal-Mart; these are tough to find, since "Wal-Mart is a formidable opponent in court . . . reluctant to settle cases promptly and fairly and almost seems eager to take cases to trial."

✪ **http://members.aol.com/walmopboy/abuse/index .html** This "Wal-Mart Employee Abuse Forum" appears to be a grassroots site. Not updated since July 1999; still, it offers plenty of horror stories and a non-union call for workers to unite.

⊗ **www.sprawl-busters.com** A huge site run by Al Norman, Greenfield, Massachusetts-based "Sprawl-Busters" consultant, which "helps local community coalitions on-site to design and implement successful campaigns against megastores and other undesirable large-scale developments." Not exclusively focused on Wal-Mart; he takes on Home Depot, K-Mart, and the like. But Wal-Mart stories dominate the always-current "Breaking News Flash" section.

⊗ **www.nlcnet.org** Site of the National Labor Committee (NLC), whose mission is "to educate and actively engage the U.S. public on human and labor rights abuses by cor-

Wal-Mart on the Web

Of course, the folks at Wal-Mart have become Web-savvy too. No fools they—seeing the fortune to be made in on-line selling, the Bentonvillains formed a joint venture with Accel Partners and launched their online store www.wal-mart.com in Fall 1999.

There's more to the site than shopping, though. With a little digging, you can unearth a rich trove of information. We suggest you follow the links from "About Wal-Mart" to "Corporate Information," then nose around. You can stay abreast of the ever-growing outlet and employee totals, check out the "Supplier Development and Proposal Guide," and delve into the annual reports. Watch out, though, for the piles of horn-tooting hooey—they can really raise your blood pressure.

porations." Full details about sweatshops (including Wal-Mart's deep involvement), NLC efforts to expose and reform them, and ways to get involved.

○ **www.users.cloud9.net/~pofn/prtkvendor.html**
This People of Faith Network site was launched for the 1999 Holiday Season of Conscience, a joint effort of PFN and the NLC. It describes the organization's "People's Right to Know Campaign: A Call for Transparency and Accountability in the Global Economy" aimed specifically at Wal-Mart. Includes a Wal-Mart Scorecard and point-by-point examples of how Wal-Mart and its chosen vendors around the world violate its Vendor Partner Agreement.

○ **www.harbornet.com/pna/WalMart/walmart.html**
With the snappy home-page headline "Us Against the Wal," the Web site of the Peninsula Neighborhood Association of Gig Harbor, Washington, documents their (successful!) fight to keep out the big retailer.

Got your armor on and your sword drawn? Here are twenty-three tactics for beating back the dragon.

Retailers

We've had scores of telephone calls and letters from independent merchants since the first edition came off the press in May '98, and we've gathered a baker's dozen of ideas you can use to fight back.

A Nixon fan we wuzn't, but let's give old Tricky Dick credit for saying "When the going gets tough, the tough get going." Remember, you're fighting one of the most ruthless big companies in the history of American business—one of the toughest of the tough. So let's get going!

Try one, try them all—and give Wal-Mart hell.

1. MINIMIZE YOUR COMPETITIVE EDGE

That's right. Limit your exposure to Wal-Mart's competition by taking yourself out of competition as much as you can. One of the smartest merchants I know emphasizes that you can't—no way—compete with Wal-Mart by carrying the same brand-name merchandise. Simply visit your nearest Wal-Mart on a regular basis and make a mental note of the brands the discounter is stocking. Then stock a competing brand.

2. THROW YOUR WEIGHT AROUND

Eleven Argentinean vendors refused to sell to Wal-Mart, citing pressure from long-established retailers who carry the same lines Wal-Mart is discounting. (Wal-Mart's response, according to *The Wall Street Journal*, was typically charming: "[We] may have to import merchandise into Argentina and take business away from local workers.") This approach may not be viable for a number of small guys, but consider your vendor relationships in this light: they may be sick of dealing with Wal-Mart.

3. JUST SAY NO

The next time you go to an exposition, ask exhibitors whether they are selling to discounters. If the answer is yes, chances are you won't get a good discount. Bonus point: if you decide not to place an order, you may want to tell the exhibitor that this was a factor in your decision.

4. USE GUERRILLA TACTICS

Check out how one of South America's biggest discounters, Carrefour, is giving Sam Hell, with a capital H. According to

The Wall Street Journal, "When Wal-Mart's new store prints a flier advertising bargains, the nearby Carrefour responds in just a few hours offering the same products for a few cents less—and the flyers are handed out at the entrance to the Wal-Mart parking lot." Hip! Hip! Hooray!

If you have the determination, the imagination, and the guts for a guerrilla campaign like this (even if it's a one-time deal, done on a smaller scale), you could poke a nice-sized stick in Wal-Mart's eye and have yourself some fun in the bargain.

5. FIGHT MARKETING AGREEMENTS THAT FREEZE YOU OUT

According to our local paper, the *Star-Telegram,* Fort Worth–area record store owner Bill Sowers launched a protest against the rock group Aerosmith in 1997. The group's label had made an exclusive deal with Wal-Mart to distribute its new EP. Feeling burned and righteous, Bill S. returned his entire stock of the group's other albums to the label. The cost to him will probably be about $1,000 to $2,000 in sales, all told, but God bless him!

For other store owners caught in a similar problem, here's a less gonzo approach: Enlist the help of your loyal customers. Publicize what's going on. Put out some fliers or a sign letting folks know of the cozy agreement between Wal-Mart and the record label—and telling them whom to write to if this ticks them off (give the label's address and e-mail).

If customers in your store were actually looking for the new Aerosmith EP (or whatever), then they'll know why they can't find it, and they might be pretty upset—but not with you. (Some of them might just go over to Wal-Mart and buy the damn thing there, but you weren't going to get that sale anyway, were you?) Your sign makes it clear who's to blame, and the label might actually get some feedback from people they listen to: consumers. There's always a hope that, shown a downside, they'll be less ready to pull this crap the next time.

6. SELL MORE SHOES

This came from a friend we were having a drink with the other night. A close friend of his has a shoe store in a small Arkansas city of around twenty-five thousand.

When Wal-Mart came to his town, he went right into their store, notebook in hand, to jot down every brand of shoes, socks, and stockings that would compete with his stock.

A week later, he had a sale on every brand that Wal-Mart was carrying.

Next, he called the shoe companies that he knew had refused to sell to Wal-Mart. From now on, he said, he'd also concentrate on odd sizes that he knew Wal-Mart wouldn't stock. He blanketed his sales area with newspaper ads that he could fit any foot.

He mailed a card to his regular customers: new lines of shoes, more sizes, more up-to-date styles than they could find elsewhere.

Wal-Mart didn't faze this shoe specialist (oh, yes—he emphasizes *specialist*) even a wee bit. He's making more money now than ever before.

7. CURB SERVICE, IN THIS DAY AND AGE?

Curb service went out long ago, you say? Not down in our part of the country (Texas).

Just a few years ago we noticed the first Sonic Drive-in restaurant on University Drive here in Fort Worth. With waitresses on skates bringing trays right to your car, it took us back to the fifties (for those who remember, that was BWM— Before Wal-Mart).

Sonics were a little slow to catch on, what with a McDonald's every mile or so. But now, gosh, there are scads of Sonics in our area—even in a lot of small towns.

This doesn't just work for restaurants. Our old friend Milton Usry had a dry cleaning business. When you pulled up to drop off clothes, one of Milton's employees hit the curb to take 'em almost before you'd stopped the car.

Not only that—they knew which customers were coming to pick up an order, and by the time you reached the counter, they would have pulled it from the rack and had it waiting for you, ready to go. If you had to wait more than a minute, they'd cheerfully carry your order out to your car.

Milton, we should add, also did an excellent cleaning job, but that curb service was the little extra something that made him the number-one dry cleaner in town.

Oh yes. Milton retired a well-to-do man. A very well-to-do man.

That little extra something. Isn't that what we're all looking for?

8. IF SAM WALTON COULD DO IT, YOU CAN TOO

We wouldn't stoop so low as to read the late Sam Walton's autobiography. So we've gotten this second-hand: When Sam first started his chain of stores in small towns, he'd disguise himself in sunglasses and goodness knows what else, visit his competitors' stores, and make note of their prices—then go back to his Wal-Mart store and have his employees make new price tags for similar items, cutting the other stores' specials.

What's good for the goose is good for the gander. Here's what some of our readers have done.

One hometown guy told us he made weekly rounds to his local Wal-Mart and jotted down prices that were higher at Wal-Mart than at his store. He had "Compare Our Prices" flyers printed up: "Wal-Mart's price for _____ is $_____. Ours is $_____." He hired a boy to stand by an entrance road to Wal-Mart, handing flyers to every driver who'd take one.

Another mom-and-pop dealer was equally brazen. He did the same kind of price-checking, then painted comparison signs on his show windows for all passersby to see.

Remember, on thousands of items at any Wal-Mart, they *do not* always have the lowest prices. Let your customers know that Wal-Mart's are **perceived** lower prices.

9. HAVE YOU EVER SEEN A WAL-MART MECHANIC?

For half a century we owned trade magazines published exclusively for dealers who serviced what they sold—fifty years for our *Bicycle Business Journal*, thirty years for our *Outdoor Power Equipment* magazine. When dealers visited our booth at trade shows, we'd generally get around to asking them how they competed against Wal-Mart. These methods stand out:

- One bike dealer had a big sign in both his front window and shop, asking "Have You Ever Met a Wal-Mart Bike Mechanic?"

- An outdoor power equipment dealer had an equally eye-stopping sign: "Wal-Mart Lawnmowers Repaired Here."

- A bike/exercise equipment dealer in Indiana was disturbed when both a Wal-Mart and a factory outlet mall moved into his town. This prosperous two-store operator opened a third store adjacent to the factory outlet mall, and last we heard, his store in the heavy traffic area was the most successful of his three-store chain.

Remember: Wal-Mart mechanics are almost nonexistent. If you sell something that rolls or has a moving part, service is your *number one* selling point.

10. HOME DELIVERIES—WAVE OF THE FUTURE?

Picking up and delivering ain't one of Wal-Mart's specialties. So many things lend themselves to this extra touch that customers would appreciate such service in these busy-busy, no-time-to-do-it-all times.

Drugstores in competition with Wal-Mart should make home deliveries, and advertise that they are able to provide that little something extra.

Clothing stores—both men's and women's—could deliver purchases that need alteration. Just like prescriptions, there's a good mark-up on apparel.

If that Domino man made hundreds of millions on delivering pizza, certainly all specialty restaurants should consider which of their foods could be delivered, hot and tasty, to the customer's door.

Yes, hundreds of Wal-Mart stores have rented space to local cleaners who expect you to drop off your clothes and pick them up. We've lost count of the cleaners in our town who probably would have stayed around if they had offered pick-up and drop-off services in our part of town on specific days of the week.

And think about pickup and/or delivery of items that need servicing (see tip #9). All those stores could increase business by offering such services.

Food for thought, anyhow.

11. HAVE A SPECIAL ON SOMETHING—ALWAYS

Way back when we were publishing the Van, Texas *Banner*, Van's main grocery store was owned by a grouchy old man, who made up in salesmanship for what he lacked in personal warmth. His store was a small, run-of-the-mill type and all his prices were pretty much the same as the other four grocers, with one exception. In the middle of his store, he always had a HUGE STACK of some kind of canned goods—beans, corn, hominy, whatever his wholesaler had on special—that he could sell for a penny or two less per can than his four competitors in town. An eye-catching sign near the entrance trumpeted "Three cans for 49¢, four cans for 69¢." That's all it took for the shoppers of Van to *perceive* that his were the cheapest prices in town.

12. IF YOU DON'T HAVE A COFFEE ROOM, GET ONE

We've seen this happen so many times that we know it works.

For some twenty years we bought all our cars from the same dealer. Seems you can't avoid twenty or thirty minutes of "haggling" time: what color, leather or plush seats, winterizing, price, terms of payment . . . Our old salesman, Al Hewitt, always took us to the company's coffee room to "talk it over." Free coffee, of course, or a soda from one of the dispensers if Al felt like springing for that much.

This coffee room bit is intended, of course, for dealers of higher-ticket items.

Higher price tags were certainly the order of the day when we went to wife Lennie's favorite dress shop here in Fort Worth, Mary McCauley's. Mary's husband, Jim, has a particular knack for making husbands feel at ease. He always met us with, "I've got coffee, decaf, tea, white and red wine, and Cokes. What'll you have?" Said in such an inviting tone that if you didn't take one or the other, you'd be insulting him. So we took. And Lennie bought. And bought. And bought.

We've been in hundreds of bike stores in our fifty years of publishing dealer trade journals; several of the more successful places offered comparable hospitality. Particularly appreciated when you remember that the better bikes sell from $400 and up.

Remember that Wal-Mart has never been known to give *anybody anything* for the sake of hospitality and good will.

Take advantage of that. Somewhere in your store there's room for it. If nothing else, curtain off a place in the back—and serve those loyal customers from a fresh-brewed pot.

13. SELL AMERICAN; BUY AMERICAN

One of the biggest advantages independent retailers have over Wal-Mart is that the Bentonville Bullies can almost be classified as anti-American in their buying of men's and women's apparel and shoes. In 1999, textile workers' unions came up with a figure of *80 percent imports* in Wal-Mart's men's and women's departments.

Every—repeat, *every*—independent dealer should look for the label on every item that could be classified as fast-moving merchandise, and run "Made in America" ads in your local newspaper on a regular basis. By all means, make that headline as big as you can—**MADE IN AMERICA**—on brands not sold by Wal-Mart. And how about a small fight-back line like "CANNOT BE FOUND IN WAL-MART STORES"?

Believe it: The more *you* play up "Made in America," the sooner American factories can regain some of the jobs they've lost to slave labor in overseas plants.

Suppliers

If you sell to Wal-Mart and they are killing you on the margin, there's just one thing I can recommend that you consider:

14. DON'T PLAY

According to *The Wall Street Journal*, the toy manufacturer Step2 has decided not to supply to Wal-Mart, joining a number of manufacturers who refuse to deal with Wal-Mart and other mega-retailers with "mighty retail clout." Apparently the manufacturers simply can't stomach the huge discounts at which the retailers sell their products (not to mention the other squirrelly things Wal-Mart does to its vendors—see chapter 3).

Citizens and Planning Boards

If a Wal-Mart or another big discounter is sniffing around your town, look out! Now's the time, when you still have power, to made preparations.

15. OVERHAUL YOUR TOWN'S COMPREHENSIVE PLAN

Check out the steps outlined by the Lancaster County Planning Commission in chapter 2 (page 26). These four steps, taken with foresight and thoughtfulness, will go far toward "Wal-Mart-proofing" your town. Warning: these steps take time and are best for those towns that don't have a fight looming on the horizon.

16. MAKE ZONING APPROVAL PROCESSES MORE STRICT

This is a corollary to #15, above. Wal-Marts are invariably built away from downtown, often in an as-yet-undeveloped area. This means that, in order for a Wal-Mart to be built, the developer who owns the building will have to get zoning changes so they can meet requirements for sewer, drainage, and traffic accommodation.

Now, some forward-looking local merchants with political clout are asking city councils to rewrite the city's bylaws to demand that any request for zoning changes must be approved by at least a two-thirds vote of the city council. This would certainly tend to make a quiet and sneaky incursion by Wal-Mart much more difficult.

17. HOW ABOUT A GOOD OLD-FASHIONED PETITION DRIVE?

This tried-and-true (and relatively easy) form of protest was recently part of the drive to keep Wal-Mart out of Westford, Massachusetts. Many of the five hundred folks who signed the petition went a step further, wearing "If they build it, we won't come" buttons in the weeks before the petition passed.

"We Don't Want Your Lousy Store!"

Think your town's too small to mount a defense against the retail giant? If Tijeras, New Mexico (population 310) can stop 'em, so can you. In July 1997, Tijeras got wind of plans for a 155,000-square-foot Supercenter, even though Wal-Mart already had a handful of stores within twenty miles, not to mention several outlets in nearby Albuquerque.

A coalition of groups organized to stop the project: the East Mountain Citizens Against Wal-Mart, the East Mountain Neighborhood Defense Fund, the East Mountain Legal Defense Fund, and the Bernalillo County government. At a town hall meeting, Wal-Mart opponents stood outside chanting "One, two, three, four, we don't want your lousy store!"

Finally, the mayor of Albuquerque swore he'd block any water or sewage lines to the Supercenter. In June 1999, Wal-Mart withdrew, having spent $300,000 on property-development studies and consultants.

Yes, Wal-Mart can be turned back—if a town or city's officials get their dander up and are willing to invest a few thousand dollars in attorneys' fees to make it all legal.

Find out your town's petition protocols, get some clipboards and pens, and enlist your friends and neighbors.

18. ENLIST HOSTS OF CALL-IN RADIO SHOWS

Does your town—or one nearby—have any call-in radio shows? They're always looking for a subject that will attract listeners. There are few souls out there in radioland who are neutral about Wal-Mart. Just think of the really juicy things you could raise hell about on a call-in show. Here's a few to get you started:

- ❂ Wal-Mart's near-total lack of support for local institutions (hospitals, churches, charities, etc.).

- ❂ Wal-Mart's notoriously frequent calls to police about shoplifters and other store disturbances. Shouldn't Wal-Mart be made to pay for excessive police calls, just as you might be charged for service calls when you keep triggering your own burglar alarm?

- ❂ All those part-time employees who work at Wal-Mart (said to be about 40 percent of the workforce). Shouldn't they be eligible for at least some of the benefits other employees are getting?

- ❂ All the smelly garbage that Supercenter grocery departments and in-store eateries generate. How do the folks living near a Wal-Mart feel about that—and all the noise that comes from those parking lots?

- ❂ Those guns Wal-Mart sells—should it be allowed to operate that department in your hometown?

19. KNOW WHOM YOU'RE VOTING FOR

In its latest annual report, Wal-Mart reports these expansion plans for fiscal year 2000: many, many new Neighborhood

"A Great Place for a Wal-Mart Store"

What a thrill to see a town say "NO!" Even a bigger thrill to know that when a vote was taken by the townspeople of Eureka, California in summer 1999, the numbers—62 percent "No," 38 percent "Yes". That's saying not only NO, but HELL NO to the Walton family.

Eureka is a fading coastal timber town with one big dream: to build a commercial port that would breathe life back into the town's struggling economy. The most suitable location is a thirty-two acre plot used by the Union Pacific Railroad as an engine turnaround until it was closed down about twenty years ago.

Wal-Mart, always cheaper than cheap, saw the site as ideal for one of its Supercenters. It promised it would come in and clean up the long-abandoned area (has your baloney radar started beeping yet?).

Wal-Mart placed Measure J on the ballot: a long, complicated proposal that asked voters to approve rezoning the industrial area for commercial use. Never mind that the California Coastal Commission had already rejected such use of the property. Wal-Mart poured over $235,000 into the campaign. They organized a "citizens" group, hired a telemarketing firm to pester area residents repeatedly, and even sent voters pro-J mailers with absentee ballots—with the County Election's office as the return address! In contrast, the victorious local "Think Twice" committee spent just $41,572.

Wal-Mart's public relations department said mournfully, "We're obviously disappointed. We still believe this is a great place for a Wal-Mart store."

Markets, 40 new stores, and 58 new Supercenters—plus relocations or expansions of 107 existing stores into Supercenters. Mind you, this is just in the United States; 90 to 100 new units are planned for the rest of the world. And in 2001 . . . who knows?

So now, more than ever, it's important to know who you're voting for in your next city election. Ask—demand—that the candidates for city council tell you, and the public, how they feel about Wal-Mart's plans to monopolize your town.

20. RUN FOR OFFICE

Jerry Greenfield, of Ben & Jerry's Ice Cream fame, did just this in his town of Williston, Vermont. He ran for city office for the express purpose of voting against a mall that would have Wal-Mart as one of its tenants. If you care enough about your town to take a major stake in the future of its development, a local office might just be the place for you to do some good work. It is surprisingly easy to run for office on the local level, and it's something to think about if you are ready to take the next step in civic commitment.

21. USE YOUR FIFTEEN MINUTES OF FAME

Artist Andy Warhol once said, "In the future everyone will be famous for fifteen minutes." Once you get involved in your local campaign to stop the Wal-Mart invasion, you just may find yourself on the local news . . . or even on the network. Be prepared. Think about what you'd say about what's wrong with Wal-Mart, why your town doesn't want it, and what ordinary folks like you can do to stop it. Don't be shy. Make the most of it!

I've had my fifteen minutes—er, seconds. It was mid-1999, just about the time Wal-Mart "invaded" Great Britain. We got an early call from the New York office of ABC news anchor Peter Jennings, asking if we'd be available for that evening's broadcast. Would we? Damn right we would! . . .

Within minutes, the ABC Atlanta office dispatched a camera crew to my hometown of Grand Saline, Texas to scan the deserted store buildings emptied in the wake of two nearby Wal-Mart Supermarts, and I had an appointment at the local ABC office for a camera interview.

My time on that night's Wal-Mart segment ran less than a minute—way less. More like fifteen seconds. Whoever edited that segment owes me about fourteen minutes and forty-five seconds of fame. But, what the hell. My old wrinkled face, my name, and the title of my book did appear on some six million TV screens on Wednesday, June 30, 1999. A glimpse of celebrity we'll pass on to my granddaughter's children.

Consumers

22. COMPARISON SHOP

I'd tell you to check prices and write them down for comparison with another retailer's, but Virginia Berger of Spring Hill, Florida, tried to do just that and was told by the Wal-Mart staff that jotting down their prices was "against store policy." Whew! Now why could that be? Could it be because study after study has shown that Wal-Mart's prices are, for the most part, not lower than discount competitors—that they are, in many cases, substantially higher?

Well, you may have to use your excellent memory (or a mini tape recorder), but if you have any doubt, find out for yourself. Most of us know to shop around when we are making a big-ticket purchase. But what about those mid- and lower-priced items? So many of us depend on ads to do the comparing for us, but there's an obvious problem with that.

If you want to determine which store or stores in your

area actually have the lowest prices overall, why not check it out? Many of you have the minor luxury of not having to bargain-hunt on everything you buy, from toilet paper to mac-and-cheese, but it would be nice to know who you can trust, in general, to be giving you a good price. And it may not be the much-hyped discounter.

Of course, it is this kind of conscious buying that Wal-Mart allows you to escape entirely. Everything all in one place! One-stop shopping! If not the lowest price, at least one that looks fairly competitive! Just remember what kinds of things you are giving away when you give away your power as a consumer to the big discounters—and what they are reaping in return when too many of us start thinking this way: massive profits and huge growth; the blind arrogance of a mighty corporation; and the ruin of the texture of so much of small-town America's commerce and society.

The long and the short of it for me is, I hate Wal-Mart. I'll never set foot in another of those emporiums as long as I live, and I'll fight them until the day I die.

You, on the other hand, may choose to shop at Wal-Mart; you may even be happy to have a Wal-Mart in your town. There are legitimate reasons to shop there and real reasons why people welcome Wal-Mart into town.

All I ask is that if you do decide in favor of Wal-Mart—whether you're shopping for a barbecue grill there or permitting the mega-retailer to build in your town—just know what you are choosing, and know what you are choosing to give up and what you may be allowing to be destroyed.

Readers

In the first edition, I invited you to chime in, and did you ever! Your calls and letters have confirmed my worst suspicions about the Bentonville blankety-blanks—and given me hope that we shall yet rise up and smite them! I've shared with you in these pages some of my favorite responses (see the "We Get Letters" and "And We Get Calls" sections at the end of most of the chapters).

I'd still love to hear from you about your encounters with Wal-Mart. Please write to me if you'd like. Just use the front and back of this page, tear it out, and mail it to Bill Quinn, c/o Ten Speed Press, P.O. Box 7123, Berkeley, CA 94707.

Former Wal-Mart Employees

Keep letting us know why you told Wal-Mart to take the job you had and shove it. Send your letter (or tear out this page, write on it, and send) to Bill Quinn, c/o Ten Speed Press, P.O. Box 7123, Berkeley, CA 94707.

Independent Merchants

Merchants who have been put out of business; storekeepers suffering from Wal-Mart's business tactics—tell us your stories! Writing on your letterhead would be great, but you can also tear out this page, write on it, and send it to Bill Quinn, c/o Ten Speed Press, P.O. Box 7123, Berkeley, CA, 94707.

Vendors/Suppliers

I know you've suffered the most financially as a result of Walton Enterprises. Write to me about your mistreatment. I guarantee that your letter will be kept 101 percent confidential, unless you tell me personally that it's okay to publish. My address is Bill Quinn, c/o Ten Speed Press, P.O. Box 7123, Berkeley, CA 94707.